CREATIVITY

Scholars Press
Studies in the Humanities

Creativity:
Lectures by Gregor Sebba

Edited by
Helen Sebba and Hendrikus Boers

Scholars Press
Atlanta, Georgia

CREATIVITY:
Lectures by Gregor Sebba

Edited by
Helen Sebba and Hendrikus Boers

Library of Congress Cataloging-in-Publication Data

Sebba, Gregor.
  Lectures on creativity.

  (Studies in the humanities; no. 13)
  Bibliography: p.
  Includes index.
  1. Creative ability.   I. Title   II. Series: Studies
in the humanities (Atlanta, Ga.): no. 13.
BF408.S386   1986   153.3'5   86-26121
ISBN 1-555-40079-5 (alk. paper)
ISBN 1-555-40085-X (pbk. : alk. paper)

Survey of Topics

Lecture One
What is Creativity?

Lecture Two
Creativity and the "Unconscious"

Lecture Three

The Silent Partner in the Creative Event

Lecture Six

Order, Complexity, Intensity:
Toward a Theory of the Great Work

Plates

Editors' Preface

In the Spring of 1983, at the invitation of Professor Robert Paul, Director of the Institute of the Liberal Arts, Emory University, Gregor Sebba gave a series of lectures on creativity, a subject that had occupied his mind from the beginning of his scholarly life. Originally ten lectures were planned, but circumstances limited their number to six. Four were taped, the first three and the last. During the next two years Sebba worked at integrating those lectures into the broader framework of a book, but this work was cut short by his death in April, 1985.

After his death a friend requested a copy of the tapes, and in the process of making copies we realized that the four surviving lectures embodied enough of Sebba's essential ideas to justify their publication as they stood. It should be kept in mind that these are transcribed, largely unrevised lectures presented in Sebba's effective oral style. References have been checked as well as possible. Most of them were cited from Sebba's memory or as freely translated titles, leaving us with uncertainty in a few cases.

The "Survey of Topics" is not an attempt to summarize the arguments but should be understood as an index, enabling the reader to find specific topics readily. It lists only the beginning of a discussion which may often continue into further topics. "The Egg of Columbus," for example, continues across several pages even though we identify two other topics in the course of that discussion.

For generous help in the project we would like to mention especially Professor Robert Paul of the Institute of the Liberal Arts, in which Sebba taught from 1959 until his retirement in 1974; Vice President John Palms, who, as acting Dean of the Graduate School of Arts and Sciences during the academic year 1985/86, provided funds for transcribing the tapes; Conrad Cherry, Director of Scholars Press, for his acceptance of the lectures in the Humanities Series; and President James T. Laney for financial support of the publication. We would also like to thank Dorcas Ford-Doward for the transcription of a text that was often complicated and sometimes obscure.

HELEN SEBBA
Hendrikus Boers

Lecture One

What is Creativity?

What I want to do in these lectures is to present some of the results of about thirty years of work on the problem of creativity. It goes back much farther, and I have to say something about that too. Basically, it was after I came back from the war that I went seriously into the problem, and the first results came very quickly, the first publication too: 1949,[1] on the occasion of the two hundredth birthday of Goethe, a long essay on Goethe, on human creativeness. The last paper, or most recent one, an offshoot of all this, was published only a few months ago. It has absolutely nothing to do with creativity but belongs to a series of papers in which the ground for what I'm going to present here is very carefully explored.

The title of this lecture, "What Is Creativity?", and the description, is not what I intended, but I was warned that my original title was not understandable, so I wrote this one, which is an unanswerable question. I cannot talk about "What is Creativity?" because I don't know what it is, and if you ask how I have the nerve to announce ten lectures on the subject, I have to say that I have been in the habit for a long time to study what I don't know. Other people study what they know, and never the twain shall meet.

My original title was simply: what is the question? because I know what the question is; I don't know the answer. Therefore this is going to be a free exploration, and today is going to be a difficult one because I'll have to say a great deal without explanation. However, in the future lectures everything that is brought up and needs really to be explained and supported will be so explained and supported.

---

1. Gregor Sebba, "Goethe on Human Creativeness," in *Goethe on Human Creativeness and other Goethe Essays* (ed. Rolf King; Athens, Ga: University of Georgia Press, 1950) 105–178.

And so today I am going to do three things. First of all I'm going to try and go into the question: what is the question? what is the lay of the land? where are we at? because that is where the difficulties begin, and the difficulties are not, I think, in the problem of creativity but in us. This is a very poor time to go into that kind of investigation, and that will be the first point I'm going to make.

I shall, then, briefly talk about the method I have used in this investigation, and then I will give two case studies, because the essence of what I'm doing is to go down to very concrete empirical problems, investigate them, and then begin to draw conclusions from them. So these two cases will be: a legendary one, the egg of Columbus, which I hear is unknown here, though it is very well known in Europe; and the other one is the question of what the wind said to the poet Rainer Maria Rilke in December, 1911, as the poet was walking up and down on the bastion of the castle of Duino. That is a very concrete question for which I have the answer.

Now let me say that the origin of the whole thing goes back very far into my own youth and in fact almost childhood. I say this because I will have to speak about a change that has occurred in the last thirty years or so and within the last generation, a change that makes the discussion of creativity very difficult. It was very clear to me as I grew up already that there was a stock of knowledge that was not out of books; it was embodied in proverbs; it was embodied in poems that everybody quoted in very flippant quotations of everything, and out of all that there grew gradually the conviction that there are some very great things, just as there are some very great men. And by the time I was, well, what you would call a high-school student, which corresponds to an American college student, it became very clear to not only myself but my friends that there were creative achievements that were so great that they were not really measurable by human standards. There were great this, great that. We had our heroes, and they were very unexpected heroes in many cases. It was not that we ran with the crowd. It was a little group: there was a beginning poet who wrote interminable poems, totally unreadable and unpublishable but well meant, and eventually he developed; there was a musician; there was an artist, and so forth, and somehow we began to separate the great things from the small ones.

And then as a university student I began to ask myself the nature of this greatness. Is it something that is the top of a scale that goes up gradually or is there something like a quantum jump where there is a level and then another level and then still another level, and you just jump from one to the other? It is a very practical question. Is it possible to raise the level of creativity in an individual, as we can raise, for example . . . as a coach takes a human being who is relatively normal, except that he is a sportsman, and develops him so that he runs faster than anybody? Is it that, or is it that there is something in the creative work and in the creator that is not measurable on that kind of scale?

At any rate at that time it was very clear that there are great things, great men, great actions, great poems, great everything, and there was no shortage of great people at the time. Now this has changed; it has changed in the last thirty years or so, thirty to thirty-five years, where, when you speak about that, you find raised eyebrows. We live now in a very democratic age, where it is sort of indecent to be somewhere where others are not and even more indecent to say of other human beings that they can't get there. Now, in this kind of atmosphere, which is basically the atmosphere of a technological consumer society, the problems that I am going to speak about are very hard to grasp and we are going to have very soon an objection on the part of our sociologists.

Now, I find that this is—I'm just going to present it as a statement, a difference, and we'll come back to it sometime—the difference between what I call a producer society and a consumer society. It is very simple. A producer society produces and keeps down consumption. In other words it's a society that accumulates savings. A consumer society is one that consumes in order to be able to produce and which accumulates debts. Why is this so? Because the producer society or the producer mentality has a very long time-range. It goes back into the past because what it deals with comes out of the past. It has a present where there are needs. These needs are measured not by the present day but by the past, and, more importantly, by the future, because the producer society produces for the future. And that is why it is these societies that leave these enormous things that stand around in the landscape: pyramids in Egypt, ziggurats in Babylon. It is the society that you find in the Bible, right in the beginning, that built a tower that wants to go to heaven. For whom? For the consumers definitely not. The consumer society is quite different. If you think of all the buildings that go up and you try to remember one that represents the present, the past and the future, you've got to look far and away and you will probably come up—oh, I don't know, with St. Peter's in Rome or something like that that we haven't built.

In other words this is a time now where today governs, and therefore we are in a situation where we think on the principle which an American airline once eternalized with the slogan: fly now, pay later. And the then Secretary of State, Mr. Dulles, who liked to fly, then became the object of another slogan: he flies now, we pay later, which was also true, you know. We are not concerned with the far distant future; we are not concerned with leaving anything for the future. In other words, we are not time-oriented any more; we are moment-oriented. And therefore the problem of greatness is very hard to handle now.

I would like to ask now: how is it possible that a mentality, or whatever you want to call it, changes within such a short time? Now, of course it doesn't change in such a short time. When you investigate it, you find that that change comes from far, far back. But there is the old saying again—and this is why I am talking about proverbs—there is a straw that breaks the camel's back. The camel's back wasn't broken because of the straw, but there comes a point where things suddenly turn over, turn upside down. So let me now ask: how is it possible, and what changes? And here I would like to show the first slide. [Plate 1]

What you have here is a set of three coins, one of many such sets found in France. And we can state the period: after the Roman conquest of Gaul, as it was called, of the Celtic France, was completed, 50 B.C., and before the great invasion of the Franks, who gave the country their name, France. At the time there were Greek coins from the Greek city states in Italy circulating, and here is one of them, which was then reproduced by the Celtic original inhabitants, and it began to look like this, and after a while it began to look like that. Now this can be read in various ways. For one thing you can say—and this is what a modern artist would say—this is the transition from representational to abstract. I would like to say that I picked this particular slide—I have other reproductions of other sets—I picked this one because it is dated 1908, this picture. It originated earlier,

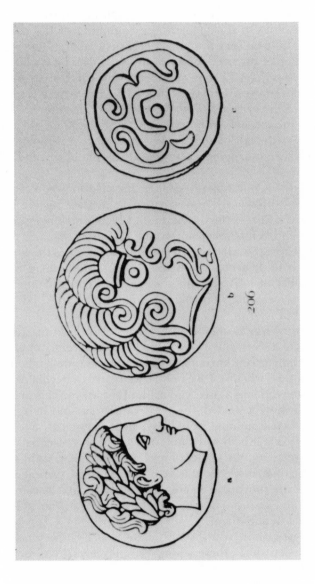

Three coins from Celtic France. Source unknown.

but this comes out of a book of 1908, and its title is *The Psychology of Primitive Art*.[2] Ten years earlier it would have been called *The Psychology of Savage Art*. This book was published during a period of about twenty to thirty years, the beginning of the century, reaching a little bit back into the last century, where there was an accumulation of discovery of art of this type. Here it is called the primitive or savage. Then it was discovered that this was also the art of children: you know, the human figure where the arms come out of the ears and so forth. And then came the third one, the art of the insane. And then came the fourth one, the art of the avant-garde. All of these have something in common, and what they have in common is to repudiate that it is primitive or savage.

Now, this is one way of reading this diagram. You can also read it very differently. You can read it as showing the disintegration of a fully formed civilization which is no longer understandable and is no longer important; it doesn't mean anything to these people. So what they see in it then becomes the eye, the nose, the hair. It becomes abstract, because the human figure, the humanity of it, is no longer a matter of concern, and here even that is lost, and then you find something that will develop into an art of its own.

The third way is to look at the series of coins in the reverse order. [Plate 2] Now the whole thing looks different. We haven't done anything except turn it around, right? And we'll read from left to right. So what we have before we read as a decline, and in this way we read it as a rise. And if I had shown you this first and said: this is how it started, then it became that, and here is the triumph of civilization, it would have been very clear. Now, you see, what I have just shown you is one way that is essential in the study of creativity: the ability to see left to right and right to left at the same time, to see front to rear, rear to front, up and down, because we are moving in an area that is not defined by concepts, is not defined by history or by anything else, and I am going to explain that in a moment.

I will now show you the next slide, which shows that what you have seen here, these squiggles,[3] develops in a very few

2. Reference uncertain.
3. This slide could not be located. It was of two single-line squiggles, a larger and, below it, a smaller one.

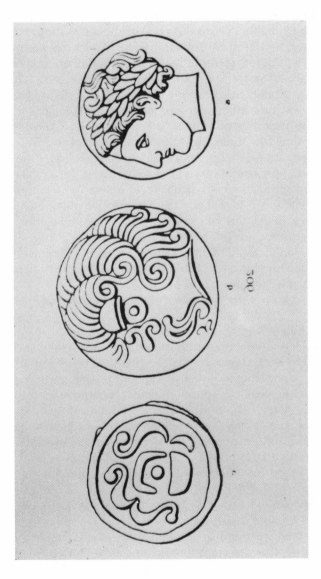

The three coins in reverse order.

centuries to an art which is exactly like these squiggles and totally different from the one it has replaced. So you cannot say that these people were not creative, but you've got to recognize that when two mentalities clash, then one of them dissolves and the other one is prepared for something else. And I maintain now that what we are going through now and what we are not aware of is that what I've shown you first, this Greek face, is an eclipse, and we are already in the state where that which before looked like a human face is beginning to look like the squiggles which may be the beginning of something else but we don't know what.

This is the first thesis; this is my explanation of the difficulty. I'm going next week to discuss what I've just done under the title of "Figure and Ground". Now, you know about the problem of figure and ground, it's the problem of gestalt theory, and I'm going to show you how intimately the creative phenomenon is bound up with this shift of focus from one thing to the other and how the whole conception, the whole structure, changes with this shift. So I'm going to draw a line here, and I'm going to talk now about something which has recently become very popular under the title "the two halves of the brain".

This picture of the two halves of the brain goes back to 1935 and is undoubtedly much older than that. [Plate 3] You know that one half of the brain, the left side, is supposed to be the logical side, the side of rigorous thought, of consistency, and the other one is sort of empty, that is, chiefly general sensations, smelling, tasting, the lower senses, except for seeing, whereas up here we have speaking, speech, memory, writing and so forth. This is the state of about 1920 to '25. In the meantime this has been investigated, and we are talking now about the two halves of the brain, and I'm going to show you what these two halves of the brain look like from the point of view of creativity.

And so we have here a division. This represents the left half—I don't say of the brain because I will not talk about physiology; I don't know anything about it, or what I know has convinced me that there is no answer to our questions in physiology, in medicine, and so on. And the reason is a very simple one. Suppose that the enormous advances that have been made in the science of neurophysiology and so forth are brought to a successful conclusion and that we know everything that it is possible to know about the way the brain functions, the way the connections from the nerves all the way down function, the

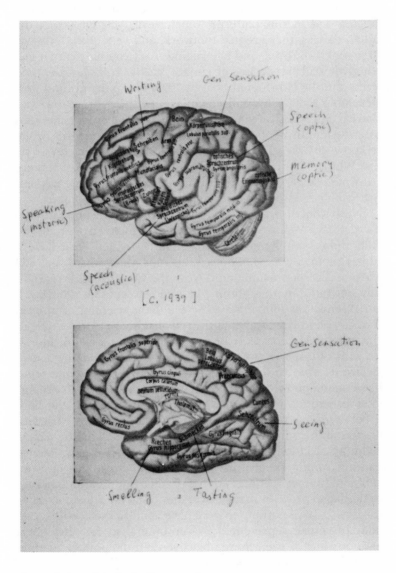

The two halves of the brain. Source unknown.

interplay between them, the chemistry and so forth, suppose we know all that as well as we know today everything about men walking, running, jumping and so on, which we know because it is a sport. Does that explain, for example, why in ancient times, in Greece, and in Rome and among the American Indians, dancing was in this pattern? You have it, you know ... the Indian dances, they are just footwork, and very quick: one two three, one two three, and alternating. And you have it in a line that gives it all away, a line of Horace, *alterno terramque cient pede,* Venus and the lightfooted Graces, "they stamp the ground with alternating foot." This dance, why is it that they did it that way, whereas our classical dance is on tiptoes, when the nervous system evidently in both cases is the same? In other words, when we know why, we still don't understand what for. Why do we do this? Why do we do that? There is no ... I don't think that there is any neurological possibility of singling out something physical that produces a whole range of quite different phenomena.

Now, what does the left side look like from the point of view of creativity? Well, you have logic and science. First of all, the main thing, you have an object-subject division. You have a subject S and you have an object, this fuzzy thing, that I shall call P because it is a phenomenon. Now, the two are separate, radically separate. There is nothing between, except that S looks at P and P sends out something to S. The basic scientific attitude is characterized by the fact that the scientist doesn't trust S. That's you and me. He doesn't trust us. Why? Because we look and we see with our senses, we feel with our senses, and the senses deceive us. And so the scientist places between the subject and the phenomenon to be observed a scientific apparatus that S now observes and upon which the phenomenon impinges, and here in between is a receiving mechanism that produces what Eddington, in his still beautiful and marvelous book on the nature of the physical universe, 1928, called pointer readings. Pointer readings cannot deceive us because pointer readings have no ambition; pointer readings are not deceived by theories that they would like to prove or to disprove; they don't fall asleep; in other words, they have nothing that we have. And so there is this wall, today of course represented by computers, so that they get a readout which is even more objective than the pointer reading because in the pointer reading you can make a little mistake with your own eyes. And this is the total divorce now from the phenomenon.

But the scientist doesn't trust the phenomenon either. And that goes back to Descartes, René Descartes, the French philosopher born 1596, died in 1650, which is a pity, because he had proclaimed that he was sure to find the way very soon of living at least to a hundred and fifty, maybe two hundred or two hundred and fifty years. Well, he didn't find it, but he gave us the four rules of method. And the first rule is to divide the phenomenon into parts and then investigate each part separately. The American language is far more violent than the French language and the Latin language, and so the American language has introduced something else; it calls it breaking down the phenomenon. Why do you break it down? Well, you break it down because you don't trust it; you don't know what's in there. So you break it down into its component parts, and in order to know what the phenomenon is, you've got to go beyond the phenomenon, and you come out with each of these component parts with a cause one and cause two, a cause three, and so forth, and then you come out with interconnections of some kind that may be very complicated, and this set of causes, then, is the explanation of what is here.

So the subject that is not to be trusted understands the phenomenon that is not to be understood by being shoved away from the phenomenon and then being led beyond the phenomenon to something entirely different. This is the way we see the world today. And what recommends it is the fact that we can operate on the causes; we can predict the causes and we can control them if we have done our job right. So, in other words, prediction and control come when you distrust the world as it is out there, when you distrust yourself, when you become completely objectivized, by means of an apparatus if possible, and when you break down what's in front of you and come to the last cause.

Now, the efficacy is not to be denied, and, what is more, the tremendous increase in knowledge is not to be denied. But where do the great insights of the scientists come from? I'm going next week to speak precisely on that, and I'm going to pick the two most difficult, seemingly difficult, areas: mathematics and physics, to investigate concretely where these insights come from. The insights do not come out of *that*. Somebody can be trained in *that* and produce nothing. And there is no question about it. The great physicists, the great mathematicians, have always known it, and I'm going to show you in one very nice example what happens to a creative mathematician who believes that this is how you do it.

It's an unusual case and I'm surprised that nobody has discovered it, but it is the case of a mathematician who says that all mathematical problems are resolved by the irrational mind, and then he has a dream where he solves a problem he couldn't solve, and then he says: I swear that I didn't have the dream but I have to say honestly that I wrote it down. Well, I'll talk about it next week.

So we are now confronted with the question, where do the insights come from? And if they don't come from the workings of the rational mind, with all the machinery that we have, then they must come from the other side. We are not talking about the other side of the brain but the other side of the phenomenon. And the other side of the phenomenon is something that looks entirely different. There is nothing determined; there are no little circles; there are no walls; there are no indefinite things; there are no breaking-downs or anything like that. This is an area of possibilities, and these possibilities become concrete as phenomena, as events, and we are part of them. We are just a phenomenon like everything else. We are not outside; we don't stand outside; we are right in it. So there are connections everywhere, and that is the way in which we can achieve some knowledge of the phenomenon. And if we find something which in some way represents itself as an object of attention, something that becomes something, there is an act that involves another phenomenon, namely, in this case, the creator. And what happens is something between them that you cannot separate out because what actually is there is only the act, the act which constitutes the phenomenon and which constitutes the creator.

Therefore the investigation on this level of creativity must take the form of a study of the creative act. We have, however, some guides. One that I'll discuss on another occasion, beginning next week, is Whitehead's philosophy, which is exactly what I have just put on the board here. The other starting point concerns the nature of the phenomenon that confronts us in this vague range of possibilities. And the term that characterizes that problem is Goethe's, who speaks of it often as *das offene Geheimnis*, the open riddle, or the patent mystery. He says: do not go beyond the phenomenon in order to understand it. The phenomenon itself is its explanation. This is the Goethean concept of symbol that pointing to itself. I am the answer. It is on one level the purloined letter of Edgar Allan Poe, which nobody sees because it is lying right here. Everybody searches for it but it's right where it ought to be, you know, so we don't see it. It says: here I am, but who looks there? It is, on the other hand, at the other level, the "I am that I am," which is the self-definition of the divinity in the Bible, as you know. "I am that I am," pointing to itself. That is the answer. And we shall come back to that too. So we are going to move in this area, and I'm going to give you in the Rilke episode a concrete example of what this peculiar open mystery looks like when it happens to somebody who has talked about it and whom we can even see in a picture.

Now let me make a last excursion before we get to our cases. I've got to talk about the words that we use when we talk about creativity. And there are two of them in the English language. The word "creativity" comes from the Latin, and the word "creator," "creature," "creation," "create," and so forth, entered into the English language after the Norman conquest with the Norman French, and more importantly, with the Latin Bible as translated by St. Jerome. Now this root here is an old root. The oldest language that we know of in which this root appears is the Sanskrit *kri-*, and we have it in the word "Sanskrit" and the word *"karma"*, which is *"k a r"*, the old root *kri-*, and it means simply "to make". I have looked through the big dictionaries, and I find no meaning other than that: "to make", which comes of course in many, many different variants.

The other word has gone out of the language and only one rest of it remains and that is a very interesting one. This is a root which—I don't know how it was pronounced, nobody knows, but it is a root, *skap,* or *skop,* in German *schapp,* becomes *schaff, schaffen, schöpfen,* and it has survived in one English word and that is the word "shape". So we have a "make" word, *kri-,* and a "shape" word, the old *skap,* or *skop,* or *sköp,* of which "shape", "to shape", the verb and the noun, the "shape," has come down to us.

Now let us look at the *kri-* word first. How did the word really get into the English language? How did it get into the other languages? It got in from the Latin of the Bible because it is the third word in the Latin Bible, beginning with the book of Genesis. *In principio creavit deus caelum et terram.* "In the beginning," *in principio creavit,* "created," *deus,* or in the Hebrew *elohim,* "God" (or "the gods"), "heaven and earth." That is how it got in. Now, what kind of creation is that? What I'm going to do now is to show you the dimensions of the problem of creativity as it develops out of language. There is one meaning of it and that's fundamental: the *creatio e nihilo,* the divine creation of things out of nothing. Let me say that one reason why the scientific view in these matters is destructive is that it teaches us to look down upon myths, legends and all kinds of things that the imagination produces. In a study of creativity these things have to be taken very seriously indeed because man is asking questions and finding answers, and I'd like to say right now without any further discussion that when I talk about myth (and here I am talking about myth in the sense that I defined in a paper published in '62, which was not original with me) myth is a story that is truer than the truth. And you will find that the same holds when I speak about the legend of the egg of Columbus: that the legend that is told is a lot better than what actually happened. Because the human mind is in search of meaning, and the facts just aren't like that; they are messy. The scientists know that; the scientists do everything to get facts pure. And I think the student of human affairs has to do the same, and fortunately mankind does it for him.

Example, the creation. God created the world out of nothing. Now, we have learned that in school, and if you go to church or synagogue or anywhere, you know that this is the dogma, and that he did it in six days. We forget about that. The people who think asked another question, and, when they asked that question, then the event of the creation begins to take on a very different cast. The question was, why did God create? He had everything; he was everything; he could do anything, everything; he knew everything; he had all the virtues. Why did he create? And that question was answered by another myth. And that is the myth of why God created heaven and earth and the rest of it. The story is best told, I think, by Jacob Boehme, the famous cobbler, shoemaker, from Silesia, who was a great mystic and thinker. But it is an old story, from very far back, and that is the story of God being aware, suddenly, that he knew everything except himself. And the reason why he didn't know himself is very simple. You can know something only—and I will come back to the gestalt problem—if you can compare it with something that is not it. If you have a black thing in a black room and you don't know what it is, you don't even know where it is or whether it is. There's got to be something against which it is set off. And God is everything and there is nothing with which he can compare himself. And now there arises in God a desire to know himself.

Now I would like to make the point as clear as I can. This desire brings order into God, because a desire is something unfulfilled, and the desire in the divinity which is fulfillment itself is a fall. So God has to fall before there can be a creation. And why is there, then, a creation? Because God must create something that is not he, in order to know what he is. He needs to build a mirror. Now what is in the mirror is not the thing that is mirrored; it's only a image. But it says, and for good reason, in the Bible that when he created it, then in the end he created man in his image in order to see, to know, what he is. Although man is not God. By the way, this is an explanation that makes it very clear that this godlikeness of man is not to be interpreted that man has the qualities of God. It simply means that he's a foil in which God can see what he is because man is exactly not that. And so with this desire there comes into action an act, and the act is in time. Now the flow of time begins and now the divine order has been broken and something new happens, an ordering in time, which is an ordering of creation and destruction, of things coming into being and going out of being, the great theme of the Greeks and so forth. So we have a first type of creation in which the whole machinery of existence is launched out of nothing and out of some kind of disturbance somewhere.

Now let us look at the root *skop, skap, shape*. What does "shape" mean? We know what it means now, and I'm going to give you out of the *Oxford Etymological Dictionary* what it originally meant: the sexual organs, and then, in the form of *geskap, geskapu,* which is the German *Geschöpf, geschaffen,* the following meanings: creation, creature, form, figure, the female sex organ, the *kri*, and destiny. This peculiar set then reduces, in the old Nordic, to the form *skop*, a condition, and the plural, *sköppen,* means genitals. Now what do we have here? We have a different kind of creation, something where things attain form and figure.

We have tremendous sexual stress on the womb, and at the same time on the *kri* and on destiny, the coming and the going. And this meaning is clearly a second level and the second type of creativity, and we can characterize it as not a creation out of nothing and not a singular act.

This kind of creation is a creation out of that which will die off, therefore fate and the *kri*. And it is not a shaping of something new but a pro-creation, a reshaping; it is change, it is life, and life is of course—as Rilke found out already in that poem that we are going to discuss—the double realm of life and death. In other words, we find now our second type of creation, which is partly order, partly disorder, which goes on and on. And we can distinguish them first as the creativity of the beginning, as an answer to the question: why is there anything at all? and then a second type of creativity within the creation, a continuing creation, an order that is based on life and death. Where, then, is human creativity? Certainly it is part of the second kind. What man creates belongs to the cycle of life and death. But highest creativity, the one that I spoke of first, does not fit that pattern. It is an eternalizing type of creativity. It transcends the living.

Whitehead puts it by saying that creativity is the category of the ultimate. Goethe calls it creation that has a divine origin, given, unenforceable and unforceable, and not man-made. But he also admits of a creativity of a lower type. Let me read you a quotation from one of the late conversations of Goethe, who died at the age of eighty-three in 1832, and four years earlier, in other words, when he was in his late seventies, spoke about creativity of the highest order. (I have translated it with slight cuts.) "All productivity . . ." (He speaks of productivity because the word "creativity" was not in the German language. It is now in the language through Whitehead; that comes after 1950; it was not then. He called it productivity.) "All productivity of the highest kind, every great insight, every invention, every great thought that is fertile and has real consequences [meaning in the real world] is under the control of nobody and beyond all earthly power." Now, Goethe, as you know, had a nickname: "the great pagan". He was not a believer in God, in Christianity or anything. And this is what he says: "Man must look upon this as an unhoped-for gift from above, as a pure child of God, to be received with reverence and gratitude. This type of productivity is kin to the daemonic." The daemonic is that power that possesses men like Napoleon, men like Hitler, yes, men like Alexander the Great, like Julius Caesar, like, oh, F.D.R. in the United States, he had it, Lincoln had it, this drive of which he says it is irresistible and does with these men as it pleases, leaving them the illusion that they will what they do. This, for Goethe, is the highest type of creativity, or as he calls it, productivity. He also knows, however, a second and much lower type of productivity. It consists in bringing the work to an end in the way of what we can call masterly craftsmanship, consciously working out the details and putting the work in the final form. For this he does not claim that it reaches into a realm that goes beyond the human. He does say, however, at the end of this conversation that even then, from time to time, there is and has to be an influence from beyond the calculating, the master craftsman's mind. And now let me stop at this point and go on to the two case studies that I propose to deal with.

The first one is that of the egg of Columbus. The egg of Columbus is, in the German language at least, a standing, almost proverbial expression. I find that Americans usually do not know what I'm talking about when I mention this expression. In the German you say: "he found the egg of Columbus" when somebody has found the very simple and very, very obvious solution to a situation or problem that nobody else could solve. The reference is in fact to a story, and I want to tell you that story in three versions. The story is definitely not true, at least I don't think it is. And of the three versions, the first one, the best one, is certainly not true, even when we call true what we find in more or less contemporary sources. The story is, in this version, the popular one, that when Columbus planned his journey, he was at a dinner, and the journey was discussed, and the consensus was that Columbus wanted to do something foolish and impossible. And there is of course a certain amount of truth in that, at least something we can understand. Seen from Spain, India is far in the East, and in order to go east you first have to go straight down south, round Africa, the Cape of Good Hope, and then go up again and continue your journey east, because there was at that time of course no Suez Canal. What Columbus proposed was to go due west and then arrive in India. This is what they considered stupid, what they considered impossible, since there was absolutely no known land as far out as anybody knew who, they thought, had ever gone straight due west from Spain. At any rate, they said, you might as well try and balance an egg on either point. And Columbus is supposed to have said: well then, let's try. And he took a egg, stood it up and bashed in the tip a little bit and now it stood. I call this the best of the three versions because it evidently shows the brilliance of an original creative mind. It shows the freedom from preconceived ideas, the ability to think through a problem and to find something the others hadn't seen. And lo, the egg stands.

However, it did not happen like that. The story goes back to a story told by the Italian Benzoni in his *History of the New World*, which was originally published in 1565; that is the earliest mention of that story.[4] And according to Benzoni, Columbus was invited, after his first voyage in 1492, to a dinner given by the Cardinal Mendoza. So we are now after the discovery and not before. And during the dinner conversation somebody said: well, after all, it hadn't been so difficult at all, it's only that nobody ever thought of it. Thereupon Columbus took an egg and said: who can set the thing up so that it will stand on either the broad or the narrow end? Nobody of course could do that, and then he did exactly what he did according to the first version of the story: he made the egg stand. Now this is not so good a version because he had already completed his voyage; had already shown that it can be done, and so the second proof of his originality does not impress us very much, to say the truth.

However, there is a third version of the story, which is even earlier than that of Benzoni, and this now shows us what the real meaning of the story is. It appears in the famous book, *Lives of Seventy of the Most Eminent Painters, Sculptors and Architects,* by Vasari, appeared in 1550,[5] that is to say, fifteen years before Benzoni, and there is no doubt that Benzoni must have known that story. It concerns the completion of the dome in Florence, the dome of Santa Maria del Fiore, where the vaulting still had to be done. Brunelleschi, Filippo Brunelleschi, who died in 1444, that is to say half a century before Columbus, was invited, together with a number of other architects, to present a plan for

4. Girolamo Benzoni, *La historia del Mondo Nuovo* (Venice, 1565); Eng. tr. by W. H. Smyth, *History of the New World* (London: Hakluyt Society, 1565).

5. Giorgio Vasari, *Le vite de' più eccellenti pittori scultori ed architettori* (1550); Eng. tr., *Lives of Seventy of the Most Eminent Painters, Sculptors and Architects* (New York: Charles Scribner's Sons, 1896).

vaulting this enormous church. The other architects considered the plan proposed by Brunelleschi totally impossible. That vault, that dome, they said, could not possibly stand. Brunelleschi refused however to show them the model that he had made that would have shown the construction. The architects were naturally angered and told him that this was unfair, whereupon Brunelleschi said he would show them his model if they could make an egg stand on its tip on a marble table. Of course they could not, and he did it. Whereupon the others said: well, well, we too could have made the egg stand like that, and Brunelleschi said: oh yes, you could have, and you could have built the dome that I want to build if I had shown you my model. Now whether that incident really happened or not we don't know. We have nothing except what Vasari and perhaps his source says. It is very likely that the story may have originated because the dome, the vault that he built over that church, actually looks like an egg with the tip bashed in.

I shall now show you first of all this bashed-in egg as it appears today. [Plate 4] Here is a reconstruction of what the model may have looked like. [Plate 5] We don't know because, as you see, there are two vaults, the outer vault which is that very bold, sail-like vault, which indeed could not have withstood wind pressure and which would have collapsed on its own were there not, invisibly inside, a construction that holds up a much shallower inner dome.

Now, this story makes a good deal more sense than the second version because here an original creator proves to the less original minds the principle that he can think of ways of doing what they cannot do, and at the same time their response: oh yes, if we had seen that, then we could have done it too. This response shows that what is easy is by no means out of the world; it is by no means different from what other brains could have very well developed, except—and that is the point—they didn't.

What I have to say about this now is, however, that we must not stop at this point in admiration of the great genius. Because there is something decidedly unpleasant about this story. I don't know whether you feel that, but I have always felt that in a sense Columbus, or Brunelleschi or whoever it is, was cheating. Honestly, if you are asked to make an egg balance on its tip, or on the broad end, then you do not think of breaking that egg, and Columbus knew that very well. So that the resistance against the

The dome of Santa Maria del Fiore.

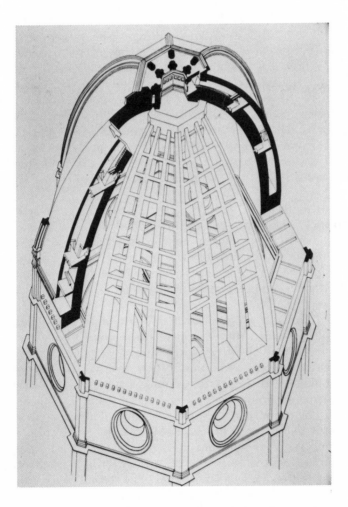

Reconstructed model of the dome of Santa Maria del Fiore. Source unknown.

creative project is by no means simply stupid, narrow-minded, etc. There is something in that resistance that is simply the insistence on the certain kind of order that is generally accepted, moving within a common understanding which the creator is trying to break out of or to destroy. And, as I say, one can very well in cases like that of Brunelleschi or Columbus say that these people who break the egg are cheating. They are violating a common trust.

Nor is that all. There is yet another side to this breaking of the egg. It is the fact that the creator, in solving the problem, destroys something that should not have been destroyed. Now, of course, eggs have to be destroyed if they are to be used other than for breeding. And there lies, of course, part of the peculiar feeling of unease that we have when we examine our reaction to stories like that. The egg is for us the symbol, not only for something that is very vulnerable but also for something that is very precious. It is from the egg that things arise. You think of the great symbolism of the world egg that floats on the waters during the period between two of those immense ages of which the Hindus speak, and you think of all the other symbolisms of the egg.

But there is still another thing. The egg is, so to speak, a hard shell, a bag that contains something living. And we too, we human beings, as you know, can be considered something that is contained in a bag made of skin, and when that bag is broken, then blood comes out, innards come out, and the being is in very grave danger of perishing. So the breaking of the egg is an act of violence.

And so let us now recognize that in this story of the egg of Columbus you have these two elements combined. The one, that there is an element of cheating, which I would like simply to suggest in connection with the fact that the inventive, the creator god in many mythologies (for example, Latin-American ones but also Germanic ones) is the joker, the jester, and the sly one, the cheater. So there is an element of dishonesty in it, a breaking of an order that is there, that is established, that works; the introduction of novelty into something where there was no novelty. And novelty in this sense is a disorder, even if it results in the creation or discovery of a new order. The second factor is that of violence. And we have to understand that the resistance against the creative work is not simply wrong. For there is indeed something that is being destroyed, there is an order that is being violated or endangered, and one cannot simply condemn those who defend this order, even though the new order may be far superior and better than the old one.

And now to the story of Rainer Maria Rilke, and how he came to write the *Duino Elegies*. The year was 1911, December. Rilke had a patroness at that time, the Princess of Thurn and Taxis, a famous family, who had given him for the winter, in her absence, the run of her castle, Duino, on the Adriatic sea. What happened on that December day, 1911, we know from the account of the Princess herself, published after the poet's death in 1926. Unfortunately, she had written it in French, very poor aristocratic French, so that we do not know what the poet actually said to her, and therefore we have to give you the story simply as a story, but that will be enough.

Rilke had to write a business letter, and I think I know what the letter was from the correspondence he had with the Princess. The Princess wanted to buy a painting from a Paris dealer. She wanted it very much, but she wanted to pay as little as possible, and Rilke was to write a diplomatic letter indicating her interest and yet at the same time showing that her interest was not too great—in other words, a quite difficult diplomatic letter. He was walking up and down on the bastion of the castle, which I'm going to show you in three slides. He was walking there, up and down, in a howling storm, walking up and down and thinking about this letter, formulating it in his mind. And suddenly he stopped. He had heard a voice in the wind saying something in good German. Since a poet always has a black notebook—at that time, a black notebook—and a pencil, he took it out and he wrote down this line, and he put it back, you know, and he went back to composing his letter. When he finished, he went upstairs, he wrote his letter, and then he copied the first line out, and it is the first line of the first of the *Duino Elegies*. And then, he told her, several other verses came immediately, and then he set to work. The whole *Duino Elegies*, ten of them, were completed in 1921–22. I should have brought my copy. It is not the first edition—I lost that—but it is a second run of the first edition.

First of all the question: what do we make of that story? One thing is certain: there is no wind in the world that speaks German. So there is already some doubt. On the other hand, has Rilke really invented that story or did something happen? Now, he was a very inventive man; he wrote marvelous stories. And it could very well be . . . he liked to sort of make something of himself. It could be, but let us assume he did not. Then what?

I want to show you Duino Castle, which, by the way, was destroyed four years after all this, during the First World War, and rebuilt. [Plate 6] This is the old Castle Duino: these crags which appear in the *Elegies;* near by is a rock. This overlooks the Adriatic Sea which is way out there. This is the new castle that goes back to the seventeenth or eighteenth century; you see how steeply it falls into the sea. And one of these windows was the window of Rilke's room; we don't know exactly which one because it was destroyed. Now here you see these windows, and you see here a walk. You see, this goes steep down to the sea. There is a little footpath, about two hundred or two hundred fifty feet. And this is part of a bastion, a wall, protecting the people who walk here. There you have a very clear view of it. One wall, a second wall, and here a walkway for the defenders; and all this goes steep down into the sea. [Plate 7]

I paid no attention to that story until one day I was reading the *Duino Elegies* and I began to wonder about the name. I read it again, and something began to stir. I knew that wind. I knew that wind. I think that there will be some—perhaps many—of you who remember one of Horace's famous odes, the one in which he warns a girl, whom he called Leuconoë, not to try to find out how many years the gods have given her to live. *Tu ne quaesieris scire quem mihi, quem tibi finem di dederint, Leuconoë.* "How much better to take it as it comes. Whether the gods gave you many more winters to come or whether this winter is the last one." *Quae nunc oppositis debilitat pumicibus mare Tyrrhenum.* "The winter, which now whips the Tyrrhenian Sea between the opposing cliffs, from cliff to cliff." The howling storm, the winter storm. And then comes: *vina liques,* etc. "In a short while you will cut short all your long drawn out hopes, your time will be up." And therefore the famous *carpe diem,* enjoy today and don't trust tomorrow.

But there you have the winter storm, and that winter storm I knew as a boy, because I grew up about seventy-five miles northwest of Castle Duino, in the mountains. From these mountains there comes down into Italy the wind called the *Bora.* And I remember it. When the wind came down, it howled, and I mean it howled and it screamed and it grabbed the shutters—all win-

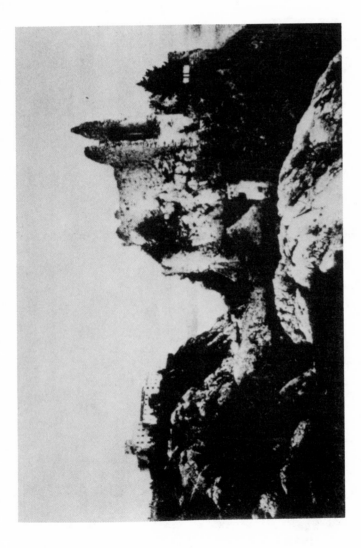

The old Duino castle. From Ingeborg Schnack, *Rilkes Leben und Werk im Bild* (Wiesbaden: Insel Verlag, 1956.)

The walkway at Duino castle. Source unknown.

dows had shutters, wooden shutters—and it would shake them like this. And there was the creaking of the weathercocks. And I remember going to school or walking with my father. You walked like this into the wind and you could hardly breathe because when that wind hits you, you can't get enough air. And when you walked home, you walked like this so that you wouldn't be blown off your feet. And I recognized that wind and suddenly I knew what had happened. The poet was walking like this, you know, and thinking about his letter, and suddenly he hears the first line of the *Duino Elegies: Wer, wenn ich schriee, hörte mich denn aus der Engel / Ordnungen?* "Who, if I screamed, would hear me out of the angel's orders?" *Und gesetzt selbst, es nähme / einer mich plötzlich ans Herz . . .* "and suppose, even, one of them should suddenly draw me to his heart, I would perish of his stronger existence."

Now, that is perfectly normal. Let me say it again:

WER, wenn ich SCHRIEE, HÖRte mich DENN aus der
ENGel
Ordnungen? Und gesetzt selbst es nähme
einer mich plötzlich ans Herz: . . .

You see where the break comes? It's in the language. This is the voice of the wind. *Wer, wenn ich schriee, . . .* It goes even into English. "Who, if I screamed, would hear me?" You see? That is the voice from the wind.

Now, why that line? This is the beginning. Here's the beginning. A poet, even when he composes a business letter, is still a poet. And a poet has a subconscious mind, and, as you saw in this picture of the bastion, he was walking in a pretty exposed position. Nothing much would happen to him because poets, particularly sensitive ones, take great care where they walk, you know. But subconsciously he was aware of that fall. And he subconsciously saw himself grabbed by that wind and hurled down, and the wind screaming, "Who, if I screamed out, would hear me?" Of course, no man; and of the angels, who? Who? There is a great literature about the angel in the *Duino Elegies;* nobody talks about that kind of situation.

Now it begins to make sense, and the sense is confirmed by the whole body of the *Elegies.* They are about man, solitary, exposed. There is a poem he wrote just two or three years before his death, left incomplete: *"Ausgesetzt auf den Bergen des Herzens*

. . . noch ein letztes Gehöft von Gefühl." Exposed on the mountains of the heart, way, way down, a last dwelling of feeling. This complete icy solitude. And the whole poem goes through this loneliness. In this very first *Elegy* it's those who died young, the children, the children. They are just beginning to learn what things are, beginning to learn what a toy is, what a house is, and then suddenly their death. And now all this is fluttering loosely in empty space, meaningless. There are the people in the church that he visits, the unknown ones who died before they even began to live. And then, in one of the later *Elegies*, the great Lament, where the goddess Lament takes the poet by the hand and leads him into the primordial mountains of death and of mourning, and there he finds water springing up, and the angel says, "See this. When it comes down to the land of men it will be a great carrying river."

This is the theme of the *Elegies*. And this is why, when he then, after he had written his letter, sat down and copied the first line, the others came as by themselves. "And even if one were to take me suddenly to his heart, I would perish of his stronger existence. For the beautiful is nothing but the beginning of the terrible, and it [the beautiful] . . . we admire it so because it serenely disdains to destroy us."

Now see this theme? "Because it serenely disdains to destroy us." That is the theme.

> . . . Denn das Schöne ist nichts
> als des Schrecklichen Anfang, . . .
> und wir bewundern es so, weil es gelassen verschmäht,
> uns zu zerstören.

I would like to close with a last comment on that passage. The hexameter, the classical hexameter, and the classical elegiac meter: hexameter and pentameter, ràm tedatàm tedatàm teda, and so forth, ràm tedatàm tedatàm tàm teda, doesn't go very well into German and it doesn't go very well into English. And so Rilke wrote this elegaic poem chiefly in pentameters, but there are places where the pentameter gradually develops into the classical full meter. And this is one place where it begins to do that: tàm tedatàm tedatàm. *Und wir bewundern es so, weil es gelassen verschmäht . . . :* we have a complete pentameter. So you can trace the inner rhythm of the poem by the way in which the— not false—but the unfulfilled meter turns into the rich classical meter. We have on that, by the way, a confirmation in a great study by Hermann Weigand, one of the great German-American scholars, at Yale, now a old man, on exactly this question.

I would like to conclude by saying that all this is not my invention, and to prove it I will now show you the picture of the poet with his little notebook. And on that we can close. There he is with his notebook, writing it down, and the only thing that is false is the beard, or what he called a beard; it tried to be a beard but it never succeeded. This was taken five years earlier, and I would like you to look at it very closely because next week I'm going to show you a picture of Rilke at the age of two and then a picture of him about five or six years later than this one, when he was forty, when he was drafted into the Austrian army during the war. He cut a very peculiar figure. I would like you to look particularly at the way he stands and the way he holds his head, because I want to show you this as an example of how, even in the bodily makeup of a creative person, his character is set from the beginning. It is something—this connection between body and soul and mind is something that you have to be able to see, just as you have to be able to shift between ground and figure. So I think with that we can close. Next week I'm going to talk about a few introductory things and then about mathematicians, about Paul Lévi, about the great Henri Poincaré, and a number of others, Einstein, and so on, and we will try to see what a problem-solving act is when you are working in the scientific mode and suddenly there is a block, and then the thing comes out by itself—the sudden creative illumination. Thank you.

Lecture Two

Creativity and the "Unconscious"

Question from the audience: Can I ask a question for clarification? You made a statement; it says creativity has nothing to do with the physical brain. That intrigues me.

Oh, I do think it has something to do with the physical brain because I've never seen a brainless creator. But I can clarify it for you. What I meant is that if we knew, if we really knew, everything that's going on in the brain, we could explain the mechanics of creativity very well, which we cannot today. However, nothing would explain why, for example, Rilke writes the *Duino Elegies* instead of inventing a mathematical problem or something like that. In other words, any mechanics can only tell you how the thing works. But here we are in a realm that involves meaning, that involves purpose, and I don't see any part in the brain where there is meaning or purpose. There is an accumulation of information; there are tracks, and so forth, but getting from there to the point where you can say: here something has been created in which you discern a certain kind of order, that is not something the neurologist would ever find out. So I think that these are two different tracks. I think we will undoubtedly gain a very great deal from the studies that are going to come; they're coming very fast now. But when you read something, the neurologist won't be able to tell you whether it is the work of a crank or a superb work of genius. That's what I meant.

This is a good question because we can go right on from there to the quotations with which I want to start. The first one is from a little book on creativity by a galaxy of entitled and double-titled distinguished professors who are Library of Congress scholars.[6] In their report they ask, "Is there any irreducible

---

6. *Creativity, a Continuing Inventory of Knowledge by the Council of Scholars of the Library of Congress* (Washington, D.C.: Library of Congress, 1981).

constant meaning to the term creativity that would allow gener-
alizations across many fields? Is it not a colossal pun [they mean a
play on words or a joke] to move from science to the arts to civic
culture to statecraft [it sounds like Emory!] and in each case use
the word creativity . . . Unless we are conscious of the possibility
of a colossal pun we shall be making connections that do not
exist." Now I can very well understand somebody saying that the
kind of creativity that has produced the Newtonian system is
certainly not the same kind of creativity that has produced what
our presidents are doing in the White House. If there is anything out there, as they say, that we can call creativity, then it has
got to be something that's out there generally or specifically, and
we have no evidence that what is out there is specific. In other
words, there is a difference, which these distinguished scholars
don't seem to see, between something that is general as a phenomenon, that you see wherever you go, and a generalization
that is something in our mind. We have a few examples here, a
few examples there, and from that you can construct a general
statement. In other words, there is a difference between a statement and a phenomenon, and I claim simply that there are
phenomena that are general and that creativity is just about the
most general of them all.

Of course, in order to support it I will have to ask the
question myself: is it not a colossal pun to imagine that God has
created college departments, academic disciplines, research spe-
cialists, and academic industries? And if he created them—in
other words, if that is where the specialization is: built into
things—didn't God sleep on Sunday when he created that, because it would be the only thing that he created specialized?
Everything else that is specialized grows out of something that is
common, and that is the general experience that man has had
from the beginning. Everything, even man, has evidently specialized out of something that didn't have all these brain cells
that do these sorts of things. We are not something that was
created specially, and to say, for example, that a president of the
United States, a poet, a scientist, and so on, are different makes
it simply not consistent with our experience as human beings.

I would, then, go on from there to a quotation of a very
different kind. This is by Dr. Samuel Johnson (one of his less
nasty ones) where he says, "The true genius is a mind of large
general powers, accidentally determined to some particular di-

rection." Here you have the same idea, you see, but in a much broader form and much closer to the evidence, to what is. The true genius (he means a creative mind, a truly creative mind) is a mind of large general powers . . . (definitely yes!) which now, he says, is accidentally determined to some particular direction. That means that the mind, the creative mind, ought to be malleable and is actually shaped by accidents.

We know that in everything that pertains to man we have these two things; that which is given and that which we call accidental. Everybody at some point or another takes a particular direction, and the only person that I know who never takes a particular direction is that nonexistent being, the so-called Renaissance man. His direction is being a Renaissance man and nothing else, and not a specialist. And, generally speaking, we have the peculiar phenomenon that when something is on its way, almost everything looks accidental, and when it is completed, when it is finished and you look back, then you ask yourself: how could it have been different? In other words, the creative work, when it is finished, has a kind of unity that almost defies the notion that it is the product of accident. And the combination of worker and work, the specific kind of maker and the specific kind of thing that is made . . . again, when you consider the whole development, that relation is one of unity and not of disunity. We can say that definitely because in every work there are flaws. At least I don't know any one without, and, since I quoted Dr. Johnson, I want to say that he says he has never read five lines of Shakespeare without finding at least one flaw in them. That happens generally. We would not see flaws if either the whole thing were accidental or the whole thing were absolutely in order. But what we call a flaw is simply proof that there is a unity that enables you to spot the point where that unity breaks down or is violated. And that is a point that every creator knows. You will find that poets, writers, painters, even musicians, agonize when the so-called inspiration suddenly vanishes and they've got to go on. I say "even musicians" because it is well known that when a composer writes a symphony and suddenly there is no more idea, then he just goes on making music until he has another idea, and nobody will know the difference. There are lots of stretches where really nothing much happens; you are just waiting for the thing to go again. So we have to ask now: why is it that in retrospect everything seems to fit, whereas when you look at somebody who is still on the way at work that is coming, then you can find all kinds of accidents, incidents, influences or whatever you want, that have shaped it and sometimes misshaped it?

So the first thing I want to do is to explore that a little bit, continuing the example I gave last week, the example of Rilke. Let me first summarize two things that I said last time. The first one, when I tried to show that when we speak about creativity we have really three things to distinguish, is covered by the myth of creation, of divine creation. The human mind asks: where did it all begin, or, if you prefer, why? This is the classical question that Leibnitz asked and after him Schelling and then after him Heidegger. That is where most people have it from: the question: why are there any things at all, why is there not rather nothing? This is the beginning of creativity, and we found that where there is really nothing, there is no motion, there is a perfect order in which nothing happens. So the question that occupies the human mind about creativity is the question: where does that first impetus come from that sets it in motion? And setting something in motion is to bring up the great dialectic contrast between order and disorder, because what is in motion is disorderly. It breaks an order and at the same time it creates an order.

From there we went to the second type of creativity, which can be best characterized as procreation: the incessant growth, springing up of things, of life, the changes in nature, the continuation of the process, each step of which is creative even if it seems to be destructive, like, for example, the erosion which simply removes whole mountain ranges. That is the second type, from which the third type that I mentioned, the human creativity, rises out. And there is then, of course, the great difference between the two. On the one hand, human creativity is also an act of procreation; it has in common with it that there is always something it uses in order to make something new. But the new is different, and I can now say that what we're going to deal with is the nature of that difference. The new thing will be a different order.

Then I gave two examples, the example of the story of the egg of Columbus, and the second one, the *Duino Elegies* of Rilke. This is what I want to continue with, specifically in answer to this question of the relation between the given and the accidental. And I'll show this with slides.

First of all, what was the problem of the *Duino Elegies?* The story was that Rilke was walking up and down on the bastion of the castle of Duino, trying to write a business letter in his mind, when he heard the voice of the wind, and he identified it and wrote it down—the first line of the *Duino Elegies*, "Who, if I screamed . . ?" the line in which we hear the voice of the wind— we hear it. He wrote it down, and then he put his notebook back. He finished composing his business letter, and then he wrote that line, copied it out, and several lines that follow. This was the beginning. And in the interpretation I said that what was going on subconsciously, or unconsciously, as he walked in this terrible wind, in this howling wind . . . he sort of heard himself fall. And there is the whole of the beginning of this *Elegy*. *Wer, wenn ich schriee, hörte mich denn . . ?* The voice of the wind. And then the answer: Nobody, nobody. We are alone, and there is no place of rest for us, *Denn Bleiben ist nirgends.*

Then he speaks of man's longing for community, for something that he can hold on to. Perhaps there will be the great beloved one who will come, but where shall I shelter her where the great thoughts go in and out and sometimes stay overnight? And the *Elegy* ends with those early departed, the children who die young, young people who died before the end, just when they had begun, in a typical Rilkean phrase, to learn, to learn life, to learn things, to learn habits. No longer to practice habits you have barely yet acquired; strange not to inhabit the earth any longer.

I did not show that the notion of fall is really in the event of the poet suddenly having not this inspiration but this sudden breakthrough, where an objective voice that he hears in the wind . . . where the howling of the wind translates into a great line, leads to a work of no less than ten long elegies, and probably the greatest work he ever wrote. I have not proved the fall, and I want to prove that today. I will prove it from the *Elegies*, and that will answer the question whether or not in this original moment the whole was there or not.

In a paper on the work of art as a cosmion I spoke of this in detail.[7] I said that with the first conception there comes what I called in that German paper *das Werkgesetz*, the law of the work.

7. Gregor Sebba, "Das Kunstwerk als Kosmion," *Politische Ordnung und Menschliche Existenz. Festgabe für Eric Voegelin zum 60. Geburtstag* (ed. Alois Dempf, Hannah Arendt and Friedrich Janosi; Munich: G. Beck, 1962) 525–540.

The law of the work is something that governs the whole process of bringing that work into being and to completion. It is silently there. Sometimes it does not guide, and these are the moments when the creator, the poet, the writer, anybody, has to fill in from experience, has to substitute. But generally speaking, it is this law that develops organically with the work and that provides it with its unity. And I ask now: is it not the same with the human being in general? Are we not born with a certain law in us that shapes us bodily: mind, soul, everything, and the environment into which we are born, and what happens to us? And is not the human life, then, a sort of working together of it all?

Taking Rilke as an example, I promised last week to show you some photographs of young and of middle-aged Rilke, in addition to the one photograph I showed. And I'm going to show you that now, from the point of view of looking at what was given with this man. [Plate 8] I asked you, if you remember, to look at the posture. Look at his legs. Look at the position of his head. It's a kind of question mark shape; the whole man looks like a question mark. And I'd like to say that we should not talk about superstitions and all kinds of other things when we look at shapes. Shapes are as determined as minds, and as persistent as minds, and while there is a lot of humbug in these things, there is the principle, Goethe's principle, that the inside is outside and the outside is inside. It is not only in Goethe; it is elsewhere too, as we shall see. But the outside tells us something about the inside and vice versa.

Now I show you Rilke a few years later, when, unhappily, the war had broken out and he was drafted into the Austrian army. [Plate 9] Well, if that were the American army, he would immediately have been identified as the so-called Sad Sack. There's absolutely no question. Just look at the position of his legs; it's exactly the same one, the same S-shape form. See the head. That's the character of the man: this helplessness, the total helplessness.

And now we go back to the time when he was two years old. Now we'll have a good laugh. The little boy with the big whip. [Plate 10] That big whip of course—it's the whip of his rocking horse—has been provided by the photographer, and it's a very peculiar, funny picture. Those of you who have read Rilke's *Notebooks of Malte Laurids Brigge*—actually the memoirs—may remember the story of the hand. Does anybody remember it, the

Rilke with his little black book, and as a question mark. From *Rilkes Leben und Werk im Bild*.

Rilke in the Austrian army. From *Rilkes Leben und Werk im Bild.*

Rilke: the child of two with a whip. From *Rilkes Leben und Werk im Bild*.

story of the hand? It's in there. Whether that is an auto-biographic memory or whether it is something that only he could have invented I don't know. It's the story of a little boy. He says he was sitting at the table drawing with crayons and he was so small—about four years, I guess—that he had to kneel on the chair to reach up to the table. And as he was doing a knight and using a lot of red, the red crayon rolled down. There was evidently a kerosene lamp on the table. He climbed down very painfully and found himself on the bear rug—one of those polar bear rugs they used to have—and it was totally dark there. He was right under the table now, and he began to grope, as you do when you have to look for something you don't see, and gradu-ally he began to see his hand, which was sort of exploring in the dark, trying to find it, when suddenly he saw another hand, an old, withered hand, coming groping toward the other one. And there was this moment of absolute horror when, he says, "I had a feeling that my hand had engaged itself, had involved itself, in something of which the end was absolutely unforeseeable." That is the look of the child who evidently dosen't understand what's going on, and he looks at that eye that looks at him.

Here we have the whole Rilke. From these three pictures you can almost reconstruct Rilke, with his greatness and, above all, with his weaknesses. The picture that I showed before—that's the Rilke who wrote a number of the unhappiest lines in Ger-man literature and poetry. Sentimental. And this is the man already in the child who is exposed. Here is a picture of being totally exposed. It has been said of Jean-Jacques Rousseau that he was a man born without a skin. I think that title ought to go to Rilke. He was a man born without a skin.

Now I would like to go on and explain how this theme of being exposed, *ausgesetzt auf den Bergen des Herzens,* "exposed on the mountains of the heart" (I quoted that line last week), and way, way down, a last human dwelling of feeling . . . how he brought the work to a close.

The last *Elegy* picks up where the first one had started, with those who died young. One of them is led by two sisters, *Klagen,* Laments. The word "Lament" perhaps is not quite the right translation but there is no better one. It means actually the stage where the outbreak of grief, the loud lament, has subsided and what remains is a deep, mournful personification of the stage of lament. The younger one leaves him; then comes the older one and takes him on into the valley from which rise the mountains of primordial grief, the grief that was once red hot and is now stone cold, and nothing grows on it. And there, in this valley, arises the spring that will become a great ship-carrying river when it goes down to the land of living. Because there is no borderline, no frontier, between the land of the dead and the land of the living; we live in both. And there that river will be called Joy. And as this point is reached, the second, older sister takes a tearful farewell, and now the dead man must make the rest of his way alone, rising and walking up into these mountains of primordial grief. And then comes the last brief stanza.

> Einsam steigt er dahin, in die Berge des Urleids.
> Und nicht einmal sein Schritt klingt aus dem tonlosen Los.

And not even his footfall resounds in this soundless fate.

By the way, I mentioned last time that the formal law of the work is a pentameter, five feet, that tries to become a regular elegiac classical meter. He's striving for the classical, and this line, *Und nicht einmal sein Schritt klingt aus dem tonlosen Los,* is a classical pentameter.

But, he says, if they, the infinitely dead, were to arouse in us a parable, a simile, a symbol, perhaps they would point to the catkins of the empty hazels—we are in late winter, early spring, the hazels have no leaves, but the catkins are already there, and when they bloom the pollen falls—the hanging catkins, or perhaps they would point to the rain that falls on dark ground in spring.

And now the last four lines:

> Und wir, die an steigendes Glück
> denken, empfänden die Rührung,
> die uns beinah bestürzt,
> wenn ein glückliches fällt.

And we, who think of happiness rising up, would feel the emotion that almost strikes us when a happy one falls.

So the last word in the *Elegies* is the word "fall." And the word "fall" is suddenly changed. There are two kinds of fall: the fall down from happiness, and the fall of happiness that strikes the ground to rise from there. Whether the poet knew that the fall was already indicated, was already given, in the first line, which he said was a given line, that which he heard in the wind, whether he was conscious of it, we cannot determine, but "fall" is the word that dominates the ten elegies, and "fall" is the word that is constantly playing between the two realms, rising and falling.

I shall now give you a quotation which will become crucial to the whole investigation, and I give it to you in two forms. In Goethe's *Faust,* in the famous, or infamous, mothers scene—it has been so metaphysically interpreted that it's almost become impossible to talk about any more, but it is the crucial one—Faust has to do something that is unusual: he has to go down to the mothers, and Mephisto is to tell him the way. And Mephisto says, "Sink down then! I might as well say: rise! It is one and the same." The notion that rising and falling are one and the same is, in my view, the fundamental symbolism of creativity. You find it far, far back, in Heraclitus, the pre-Socratic Greek thinker, around 500 B.C. The way up and the way down are one and the same, *hodos anô katô mia kai hêautê.* And if you look at the *Four Quartets* of T. S. Eliot, you will find that one of the two epigraphs is the quotation from Heraclitus. And when I see that then I know there is going to be one part which is the pure creativity symbolism. And it is.

I want to conclude this part by asking: what is there to this sudden reversal of falling and rising? How can you say it is the same? If you understand that, then you will immediately understand why you cannot deal with the problem of creativity by a logic or a way of thinking that knows only one thing, that allows only one thing, because it will not allow so-called contradictions. When you deal with creativity, you are constantly dealing with things that look like contradictions although as phenomena they are not, but when you put them in words: "the way up and the way down is the same," then you have either an equivocation or a contradiction. Why is this? It is for a very simple reason: because the creative process pushes beyond the knowable towards the unknowable, and this is the source of what novelty there is in it. There is a realm of what we cannot know in the usual and, in our time, the scientific way, and these contradictions arise at that point. We are, however, already investigating these contradictions, and now I'm going to show you in what way. You see here that famous white candy dish. [Plate 11] When you look at the black, then you see it as two faces looking at each other. Which is it? This is the well-known illustration that you find in every book on optical illusions: you find it in every treatise on gestalt theory.

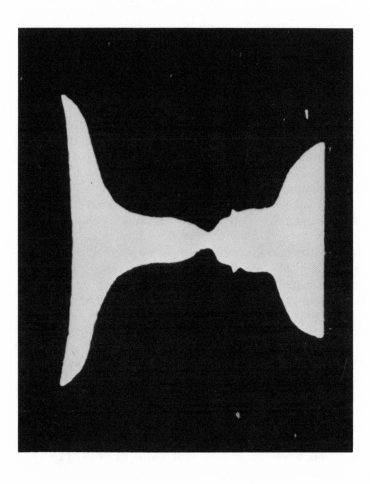

The candy dish.

If you look at the white, then you have a candy dish on a black ground. If you look at the ground, you have two faces on a white ground. What is ground and what is figure? What is falling and what is rising?

Here we have something that is much simpler. It is a flowering branch on a grayish background. [Plate 12] This business of the background is for us very familiar. We concentrate on figure and we try to isolate the figure in order to understand it, like this branch. But then, when you look at the background, you feel that there is something missing. We need to fill in the background so that we know where the branch comes from, what it is connected with, what grows around it, etc. And this is why the word "background" and "filling-in-the-background" has become such a popular way of talking. You hear a story and the first thing you think is: somebody ought to fill in the background. Right? The background, however, is not what you want to know. What you want to know is the story.

This is a Japanese painting, and the Japanese would look at it very differently. Let me quote from Don Ihde, a philosopher at Stony Brook. In our traditional way, the subject of the painting is the branch; the background is merely empty or black. Yet the emptiness or blackness of the Japanese painting *is* the subject matter of the painting. The branch is set there to make the openness stand out. That is the difference. I would go farther than he and say the branch is set there to make the emptiness visible, but the emptiness is the subject of the painting, and not the subject that you see. In this, says Ihde, there is a radical reversal. The foreground is not dominant; the background is not recessive. To understand such a painting calls for a deep reversal in the noetic context, in the context of knowing.

Instead of discoursing on this I want to show some more of it. First of all, here is a very famous Chinese painting, and if you look at it, you wouldn't know what is the subject. [Plate 13] The subject becomes a little bit more visible when you look up here. You see something triangular which doesn't quite fit the rest of it, and you see that it is a mountain village emerging as the fog begins to settle. The cloud has come down, and here is the mountain village coming up. And when you focus on these two little scribblings here individually, then you see that these are two men climbing up to the mountain village, their legs still partly shrouded in the fog. We have now converted the Japanese

Flowering branch. Source unknown.

Painting of a fog. From Hugo Munsterberg, *Zen and Oriental Art* (Rutland, Vermont—Tokyo: Charles E. Tuttle, 1965).

painting into a Western painting; we have two men climbing up
to a mountain village, and the mountain village is there. But the
two men are only there to show you what Rilke wants to show
you: two men lost in a fog. The fog is it. And here you have a
detail. [Plate 14] You will immediately recognize which one it is.
It's that spot down here. And here you can no longer distinguish
what is ground and what is subject.

Now, I say that what you have seen here explains to a large
extent the way in which the creative mind works. A mind that is
incapable of seeing the ground as figure and the figure as
ground will have certain roads closed to it, the roads that come
from a complete reorganization of everything although nothing
has changed. I'll make that point again: *although nothing has
changed.* Reordering, which goes almost automatically, as when
the poet sees things hanging, those catkins, and he sees the rain
coming down, and suddenly the happiness that rises and that
falls are one and the same.

The Japanese garden, which some people call a rock garden,
which I prefer to call a sand garden, is another example of this
kind of thinking. [Plate 15] You will not understand it if you look
at it as if it were something that some happy artist has left behind
on the Emory campus, namely, a bunch of rocks that sit there to
be beautiful. What you notice is that there is nothing growing in
this garden, and you see also that it is raked. For a Japanese you
have the raking and you have the rocks. The rocks are only there
to show the sand, not vice versa. And why is the sand raked?
Because the sand is that which is immovable; the rock is not. The
sand is immovable; it's there although every footprint changes it.
When the wind blows, it changes; when it is raked, it looks
different. The rock doesn't change, but the rock is not it. The
symbolization, the meaning of it, is in the sand. And why is it
raked? Why is it raked every day? It is raked, not because the
Japanese are very orderly people—they are; they are like Western housewives; they can't see anything lying around; it has to be
moved; so every morning it has to be cleaned up—this is not the
reason. The raking every day is a symbolic enactment of the
unity of man with the lasting, with that which lasts, which is
nothingness. You do that knowing that it will not last, and that's
what you are here for. It's the paradox that explains existence,
and it is enacted every day. It doesn't prevent anybody from
walking there, because leaving tracks is also part of life. And

The two men in the fog. From *Zen and Oriental Art.*

A Japanese garden. From *Zen and Oriental Art.*

then to eliminate these tracks and have the primordial starting point again is also part of life. So you see how this change of ground and figure, gestalt, is embedded into this view. We can now say a last word about this phase of the creative work. The deeper a creative mind reaches down into this realm where things are never the same and yet always the same, where there's constant change and yet nothing is new . . . the deeper a human mind plunges down, the greater his creative power and the more surprising the results that he comes up with.

This is a natural stopping point, and now I would like ask you, shall we go on to little Gauss or would you like to discuss some of it or ask questions?

Question from the audience: Can you give us an example like this from Western art?

Oh yes, if you have seen paintings of Mark Tobey, for example. Well, have a look at it. There are books in the library on Mark Tobey, and it could very well be that the art history department has something. He is one of those who make a big canvas, and you see almost nothing, but sometimes it looks like a figure, and then you look at the ground and it looks different again. And, as a matter fact, remember that Japanese art has influenced, and profoundly influenced, Western art, especially Western painting, from about the 1880s or 90s, and it took some time before people realized what we were picking up from there. But there are whole schools of painting, when you look back to it, which are based on the idea that what you show in the foreground is only there to make you aware in some way of what is really in the foreground, namely, the background, instead of having a thing *put* in the foreground . . . the classical Greek idea: put it in the foreground and everything else recedes. The clear division—this is what gives the great power to Greek art and Greek thinking and so on: that what you see, what you hear, is grounded in itself and stands there independently, and everything else is the background against which you see it. The Japanese, and in general the East, have a feeling for this as a kind of way of life, and especially a creative way. This is why you, then, get these paradoxes, where one of the examples of holiness in Buddhism is the scene where one of the holy men is discovered in winter by his abbot burning a statue of Buddha to keep warm. And of course there is great outrage, and he laughs and says, "Well, where is the Buddha now? I feel warm." That's the greatest tribute to the Buddha that you can pay. One could go on—the difference between this kind of thinking and creative thinking and our kind. It is not the kind of thinking that is designed to give you the precise information on this and that. And that doesn't mean that these people are incapable of it. I think the Japanese are outthinking us in our own Western way right now—and very much to their detriment.

Question from the audience: I may be committing a democratic heresy here, but it seem to me that creativity—you've been going at it from the point of view of the extraordinarily gifted person, but it seems to me that creativity is an experience that everybody has, which in fact is unavoidable. That is to say, when you seek, you are expressing something, and it has to be creative. There is no algorithm, so to speak, to begin with, given to you; it comes from somewhere; it comes from nowhere.

Ja, I would agree with you, except that I think there are some people who do extremely well in suppressing it. I mean, there are people who make a business out of that, and you have whole cultures that do so. You have to remember that anything creative is disorderly, and there are whole cultures that try to keep things on a even keel. Our civilization happens to be one which lives on innovation and therefore runs from one trouble into another. We deal with that on the principle of subject and background by saying that what we achieve is the gestalt, and what doesn't function are side effects, background. From another point of view the side effects are probably much worse than the good which we achieve with the main thing. In other words, we take the risk of being in constant upheaval because we overdo that aspect of it; we are killing things off.

I would like to quote, since I've got Rilke right here, his own comment. Rilke speaks about that in a letter from his last years— this is the famous letter to the Polish translator of the *Elegies*—on the meaning of the *Elegies,* where he says: we are here to experience the world as it is and then to transform it. And then he says, "Transform? Yes, for our task is to stamp this provisional, perishing earth into ourselves so deeply, so painfully and passionately, that its being may rise again 'invisibly' in us." And then comes this famous sentence: "We are the bees of the invisible." *Nous butinons éperdument le miel du visible, pour l'accumuler dans la grande ruche d'or de l'Invisible.* "We are the bees of the Invisible who accumulate the honey of the visible in the great beehive of the Invisible." In other words, the *Elegies* show the agitation of our own nature (and by this he means the waves that pass through us) which introduce new vibration-numbers into the vibration-sphere of the universe. And, as he asks in the *Elegies*, are we perhaps there simply to say: "tower", "jug", "gate", but to say it in a way in which it has never been said? That is to say, to take what is temporary and make it permanent in art.

And here he speaks about what is now vanishing. (Mind it, the time is 1925.) All this is particularly important because of "the ever swifter vanishing of so much that is visible, whose place will not be supplied. Even for our grandparents a house, a well, a familiar tower, their very dress, . . . was infinitely more, infinitely more intimate: almost everything a vessel in which they found and stored humanity." In other words, there was a direct relationship to things, and in a civilization where there is this direct relationship to things, there is the urge to preserve, the urge to keep it, to transmit. That's where tradition really means something. And this is not favorable to the kind of hectic creativity that we have, that we foster. And then he says, "Now there come crowding over from America empty, indifferent things, pseudo-things, dummy-life; . . . A house in the American sense, an American apple or vine, has nothing in common with the house, the fruit, the grape, into which the hope and pensiveness of our forefathers would enter. . . The animated, experienced things that share our lives are coming to an end and cannot be replaced. We are perhaps the last to have still known such things." What we have here is a testimony to a change in the culture, the one to which I referred last time when I spoke of the change from a producer to a consumer mentality, and that is bound up with that. So that is the answer I would give.

Yes, potentially everybody is creative, and I would say that when it comes to action, then the uncreative people are very often far more creative than the creative ones. People have a way of acting creatively not through the mind, but through their whole being. And the way they do things and the fact that they do them—in that sense, yes.

A question from Dr. Alvin Boskoff, Professor of Sociology: That brings up a very interesting and disturbing thought: that while the creative processes are apparently available to everyone, there are a couple of ways in which people respond to these. One, as you say, is the action, which means that people very often abuse their creative possibilities or exhaust them. In the other response, I think in your example, people, instead of using action, use symbols, and symbols enable them, by their flexibility and ambiguity, to make the kinds of contradictions and variations of contradictions that could be recorded. Now, action disappears, but these are recorded, and the question that I would raise is: what accounts for—this is a nasty question, of course, and probably cannot be answered—what accounts for the fact that some people of some periods and some cultures emphasize the active part over against the symbolic part of it (assuming that they are not completely exclusive of one another)? What enables people to evaluate the fruits of these according to some set of standards, so that we can say that it's creative and not just some aberration of some sort or another? It seems to me that what you are suggesting is that if people are trained or encouraged to be exploratory, not simply in action, but exploratory in thought—and that's apparently what education is supposed to be for, although most education is far from being creative or exploratory—then you can get something like creative thought. But the thing that bothers me most of all is that we're taking your assertions and others' assertions that these products are in fact created rather than being peculiar or extraordinary or whatever, and that causes me all kinds of difficulty. The processes I can understand, but the judgments of the products are open to all kinds of differences of opinions.

Ja, I know this is a problem that is very, very serious, and it can be stated very simply. There are really two problems. Let me answer first to the first. In the first you speak of times and peoples, etc. who do not create these great things. However, they do create, and they create everything that enables anthropologists to make a living off their art. Almost everything that these people have created is as individual as are the works of great individuals here. And when it comes to action, just think of the Roman example—not of the real Romans but of the legendary Romans. What they did in this or that case was the great example, right into the French revolution, where the French, who were the least Roman of all people, acted if they were old ancient Roman heroes. It is the action that stands there and that passes away, but what remains is the memory of the action. And that is, from the point of view of the history of culture, the great thing—the memory of the action. And in the memory of the action you see what you said you find so difficult with our time: these things, like in Rilke, which go on in the mind. But the stories of actions—the original stories of action—are such that you never know whether they are dealing with a human being or a superhuman being. That's exactly the same thing. The original hero, the founding father, was an ordinary man. Remember that little example that Lévi Strauss gives about one of his Australian tribes, where they piss crouching down, men and women alike? And he asks the chief, why do you do that? He says, "Don't you know that when our ancestors went through their cave they had to relieve themselves, and they couldn't stand up, and since then . . ." In other words, you no longer know in what realm you are. This is exactly what happens in modern poetry, in ancient poetry, everywhere. And if you want the work that stands in the middle, it's not Homer; it's Virgil. Because Virgil is already aware of the fact that he's not telling a myth. He is also aware that he's not telling history.

The second question that you raise is one to which I hope we will come back. It is simply that Shakespeare, after his death, was a nobody and remained a nobody in England for quite a while. He was really discovered outside England, with a new wave of understanding, and then it went back to England, etc., etc. There is no way in which you can objectively say that this is a great work or not. How do we deal with that? We can only deal with it when we ask ourselves: what is time and what does time do? Because everything that we are discussing is in time, and here we are confronted with the naked problem of time. The problem is such that some people, Goethe, for example, could say: this is something that I will not even publish in my lifetime because it will just be torn to pieces and laughed out of court, and it may take a hundred years or more before it is understood. And he was absolutely right, almost on the nose. So one can know that. And we know that we lose; every time we pick something up we lose something else. Again a quotation from

Rilke: *Wer der Erde kennt die Verluste?* "Who knows the losses of earth?" We live on the things that we can appropriate, and we lose or destroy what we cannot appropriate. And so we have to find a way of understanding what greatness across time is, and the only way I can find is to show what it has to do with order, because order is something that we can can conceive of, and we conceive of the dialectics between order and disorder.

Question by Dr. Robert Falkowitz, Mellon Fellow in the Department of Religion: I guess I'm not sure why you set up the opposition between the concept of creativity in Rilke and the Oriental concept. What seems to me is that you set up Rilke as a strong man, and you're taking this very private view of the creative process, something very romanticist. You've been quoting Rilke and Goethe . . . you put Rilke out in the storm like a Wallenstein or a Werther. And then you've taken a view of Greek art which I think is more a romanticist view of Greek art than a Greek view of Greek art. And then you set that in contrast to this sand garden and try to contrast a Western view of what the subject is and an Oriental view of what the subject is. But I think what you didn't say about the sand garden is that the person viewing it takes his place in the circle of rocks as if he is one of the rocks, and you have to have a viewer in there who is also a rock. I'm not sure that it's really a question at all of Eastern versus Western so much as a question of a very limited sort of romanticist view of creativity as opposed to a more social view. I think that there are certainly a lot of Westerners . . . you don't seem to like musicians . . .

Oh, I like them very much, but the trouble is I can't do much with them because they don't talk; they write music. That is why. I think there is a little misunderstanding here. I did not put Rilke in the classical Greek tradition or anything like that and oppose him to the Japanese. On the very contrary, what I was trying to show—and which I evidently missed—was that in the *Duino Elegies* you have a beginning that seems to be straightforward, but in the end you find exactly this reversal between ground and figure. It's right in Rilke. So, from what you say, he belongs with the Japanese and not with the West. And I said in effect that you will find this in almost every creative mind of a high order—this ability to change over.

I will simply comment briefly on what you last said because

it's important. You can of course explain a lot of things socially, and that is a very powerful way. It has only one drawback: you cannot explain society socially. You have to accept it as given if you want to work with it as an explanation. You have then to ask yourself, when you come to the basic things: what is society as seen against the great life processes: coming into being and going out of being, man maintaining himself, changing, and at the same time trying to hold on to what is, etc., etc.? So there are categories that are larger than society, and I think that we can get much farther in the exploration of this type of problem we are dealing with if we do not take the specialized explanation, whether it's sociological or whether it is psychological or neurological or any other thing, but look at the phenomenon. And when we look at the phenomenon, why not look at the big phenomenon, because we see more in it?

Follow-up to his previous question by Dr. Falkowitz: I guess my question is: I think you seem to be taking a specialized point of view by understanding creativity as this very private personal act, and, in particular, I think you're taking a romanticist point of view.

Well, I wouldn't mind taking a romanticist point of view because I see nothing wrong with romanticist points of view, except I don't think it is a romantic point of view that recognizes large lines of meaning, of understanding, that go through millennia of history. I don't think this is romanticism. If it is, it's all right too. There's nothing wrong with romanticism; there's nothing wrong with classicism; there's nothing wrong with any -ism, except that they are all subject to investigation, and they are not tools of investigation themselves. The fact that people have put things in romantic language does not depreciate what they say. They could have said it in classical language; they could have said it in Oriental riddles; they could have said it in myth, and they did.

All right, so we have ten minutes, and in these ten minutes we are going to deal with little Gauss, who is a very different matter. I want to go on to the problem of creativity in mathematics, for the reason—and that will perhaps be part of the answer—that there is nothing romantic about mathematics. Mathematics and logic seem to be the one field where the creative mind really hasn't got much leeway, so to speak. There are criteria: it has got to be consistent, it has got to be logical; everything has to be proved, and when you do something new, it has to fit in with something that has been done in mathematics from the beginning of the world and is still known today. That's a pretty big thing.

Let us look how a mathematical mind works. The mind I want to deal with is the mind of little Gauss. Gauss, the famous— well, I almost said mathematician, but if you read the celebrated eleventh edition of the *Britannica* you will find a long article on Gauss where the fact that he was a mathematician isn't even mentioned. That's time, you know. Today he is honored by the physicists, who have a physical unit called a gauss, but his great glory is in mathematics. His talent showed very early, when he was a little boy in school. The teacher, whose name we know, gave him, gave the class, an assignment to add up the numbers from one to sixty. They had to write the result on a slate board and put the board down on the teacher's desk, upside down so that the next boy couldn't see the previous one's result and pass the word around. I don't know why he gave them this assignment. Perhaps as practice in adding; perhaps because he wanted a little bit of rest. At any rate, he gave the assignment, and suddenly little Gauss wrote something down and came up and put his slate board on the desk immediately. And then the other boys gradually came up, and when the teacher read them back they were all wrong except for the last one, and he had found it immediately.

So the sum of the numbers from one to sixty is 1830. How did he do it? He figured that one and sixty makes sixty-one, and two and fifty-nine makes sixty-one, and then of course it goes on; every pair will make sixty-one. And since there are sixty numbers there are thirty pairs. Thirty times sixty equals 1800, and one times thirty is thirty, so it is 1830.

All right, here's a young man of nine or ten or eight or something like that, who has talent. The talent was reported, and the Duke of Hanover took care of him. (His father was a poor bricklayer.) He sent the boy through school. He went to the university and became a great man. What did he do? I'll do the same kind of analysis that I did with the egg of Columbus. First of all, it is very evident already that little Gauss, small as he was, again violated something that was unspoken but expected. The assignment was to add these numbers, and he didn't. If the teacher had asked him: why didn't you add them? he would have said: but I did add them, they are all in there. It's like the bashed-in egg that will stand.

I didn't realize that one can almost bring proof of this, but one of my neighbors came one day. Her son had gotten a C− on a math test where he expected at least a 95, and yet all his answers were right. Should she go and talk to the teacher? And I looked at that thing and I said yes: go and talk to her, but she will tell you that he didn't do what he was supposed to do. He got the right result, but he did not follow the procedure, and I wanted him to follow the procedure and not get the right result.

So, you see, there is a element of rebellion in there. But far more important is the way he did it. And when you asked what is so unusual about getting this kind of result, it is that the sequence of numbers, like the business of the egg, has a very significant meaning for us. You probably don't remember how you learned numbers—I don't either—but you see it in children. Children are very proud when they can count, and how do they express how much they can do? "I can count up to five," and the other one says," I can count up to seven." That is how you learn, by counting *up*. You don't learn to count down. Counting down is difficult. If you try very quickly in your mind to count back from 361 to 227, you will find that you slow down like a car where something is burning out. Why is that? Why do we learn the numbers upward and not backward? Well, you can say it's cultural or whatever. The fact is that experimental psychological tests have shown a slowing down of the process in counting down. Only with these space events where we have a countdown has the counting down become popular, but it has still not become easy.

What this boy did was something unusual. He counted up and he counted down at the same time. And in doing so he discovered that there were two orders, or knew that there were two orders, an ascending and a descending one. And he found that these two orders are symmetrical, and if they are symmetrical then one instance is enough. One and sixty is sixty-one. From then on he didn't have to say anything because if he goes up and goes down it will always be one step, so every number going up increases by one and the other decreases by one, so you always have to get the same result—evidently. Right? And he could have come up with the formula if he had known any algebra or something of that sort. Right? But that step he could not take because he didn't have the instrument of algebra yet.

This is something you can call a creative mathematical invention or you can call it a case of problem-solving. I would like to make the point that there is a difference between the two. When you have a mathematical problem or a physical problem or any other problem, then you can look for an easy way to do it or simply for a way to do it. We all do that. We do it in big things; we do it in small things. We are operating within an order we know. If we have a gadget that doesn't work, we have some idea of what might be wrong and we try it out. But we do not try to think in a different order from that which is represented in the thing we want to fix. And there is the difference. What little Gauss did was not operating in the order which he had learned: counting up. He was thinking in a different order, where the numbers are divested of direction, a number order which is a pure number order and orderly in as much as it's integers. Everything changes by one. So he must have had the intuitive understanding of what is known as the foundation problem in mathematics.

The foundation problem in mathematics is: why, when you say one plus one is two, does it follow that two and one is three and so forth and so forth? You know that there are schools of that. Once you conceive of mathematics like that, then one area of mathematics opens up, namely, the area of number theory. And you have here the example of a small boy who has opened it up. He finds the result immediately on nothing except a different conception of number order in his mind. And that, then, is the next thing that we are going to deal with. A week from now I'm going to deal with the problem of order. I'm going to apply it to the most important work on creativity that, in my opinion, has been done, as far as profitable study goes, concrete study, the work of the French mathematician, Henri Poincaré, who was no romantic, I assure you. Poincaré, who observed the creative act in himself and in others, and who found that there are four stages of it in the case of the insoluble mathematical problem which is then suddenly solved after a period when nothing works. And this not because a new gimmick has been found but rather because a new order of things has been discovered. And so that problem will then resolve itself: how does the human mind discover a new type of order or, as in mathematics, create a new type of order?

I'd like to say that there are two books that are very useful here, two that I would recommend for the two different things they show. One is Polya, a Hungarian mathematician, who wound up during the second world war in Princeton and was very much concerned with the teaching of mathematics—and that means teaching the teachers of mathematics—and who, as a result of that, wrote a book called *How to Solve It.*[8] It's a book that is absolutely a model of how to go about problem-solving in general, turning things upside down, and this, that and the other. That will explain to you what problem-solving generally means, not only in mathematics but in science, in scholarship and so forth.

The other book that talks about the problem of order (without mentioning it, by the way) is by a Frenchman, a mathematician, who also wound up at Princeton at the same time, Jacques Hadamard. It is called *The Psychology of Invention in the Mathematical Field.* Here you have a wonderful summary of the work of psychologists, of the testimonies of mathematicians and physicists, on the question of creative mathematical invention as opposed to the simpler problem of problem-solving. And I would like to say, if there is a mathematician by chance here, that mathematicians do not make that distinction. Mathematicians call it all problem-solving. What they don't recognize themselves is that some of this problem-solving is not the solving or a problem that isn't there; it is the creation of a problem. And then they solve it if they can.

8. George Polya, *How to Solve it: A New Aspect of Mathematical Method* (Princeton: Princeton University Press, 1945).

9. Princeton: Princeton University Press, 1945; Dover paperback, New York: Dover publications, 1954.

Lecture Three

The Silent Partner in the Creative Event

Today I will speak about the creative act, chiefly with regard to Henri Poincaré, the French mathematician. I would like to begin with a comment that was made after last week's lecture, where I talked about little Gauss, the story of the little boy who adds up the numbers from one to sixty immediately. I interpreted this as meaning that he had found the theorem where the sum of natural numbers from one to n, or any such sum, can be computed by the formula (n x 1) + (n + 1) ÷ 2. After the lecture somebody commented that he would doubt that interpretation because Gauss was a lightning calculator—and he was.

This is important in connection with Poincaré, who points out that mathematicians normally are lousy calculators, and that a case like Gauss, who was a brilliant mathematician and a rapid calculator, and a precocious and efffective one, he says, is the exception and not the rule. When I was a statistician, I noted among the statisticians I knew that the ones who were theoretically active were very poor at working with figures. I personally have absolutely no ability; I can't add up three numbers without making two mistakes. So, when you look at this objection, then I would say first of all: the case of little Gauss is one of those stories which badly needs improvement. It is a story which is truer than the truth so long as you omit any reference to actual fact. It is a symbolization, and we should not be blinded by fact, that is to say, fact that is not relevant. But any objection of this kind is worth pursuing because any objection of this kind leads into the questions that we usually pass over.

I began to ask myself for the first time in my life what is going on in the mind of a rapid calculator. If somebody tells us to add up the numbers from one to so and so, then we think you go: 64 plus 65 plus 66—iterative, one thing after another until you reach the sum. A human being who can do that so quickly that he takes a very complex thing and gets the results within seconds would have to have the mind, not of a human being, but of a calculator, of a computer. And is the sum of certain numbers that follow each other in a given sequence really a one-way street that you have to travel from one end to the other in order to get the result? Or do these people live in a mental world where the relationships between numbers (one of the great secrets or mysteries in mathematics, and mathematicians think that number theory is among the most superb parts of it) . . .? To live in this domain, and to know your way around almost instinctively, enables you to find all kinds of short cuts, which other computing people also find and teach. I used to teach these short cuts to students who were brought up on the American principle that the longer you drag out the computation the safer the result will be.

But people who live in that world, how do their minds operate? Not consciously but subconsciously. And the domain of the natural numbers and of the integers is particularly interesting. I need only quote the famous statement of the German mathematician Leopold Kronecker, who, when faced with the latest developments in number theory, cried out, "The integers, God himself has made them. All the rest of it is man's handiwork." That is the voice of a mathematician who realizes the exceptional position of this series of numbers.

Now, behind that question, what is going on in the mind of this calculator is the other question about the order within that domain of the natural numbers. And that order is evidently not just an order but a complexity of orders. There are orders and orders and orders, and they come together, and there are gaps between them, and you then get these extraordinary things that are the great puzzle of modern mathematics. Like Fermat's theorem, which, as you may remember, was found after his death in the margin of a book on the equation of Diophantes, where he said: I have found a very beautiful theorem, namely, that the equation $x^n + y^n = z^n$ does not hold if x, y and z are integers and if n is larger than 2. I now come back to this equation. Underneath he wrote: "The margin in this book is too small to set down the proof." And the proof hasn't been found yet. There was an enormous prize of 5,000 marks given for the discovery of this proof. Today that 5,000 marks wouldn't even buy you a typewriter in Germany, but anybody who finds this proof would certainly have more success in life than if he got the Nobel Prize, there is no question about it. And we still don't know how Fermat found it.

Then you have the other problem of the order of the prime numbers, and now with the computers this has been tested and tested and tested, and we know what works and what does not work, and we still don't know why. In other words, this is not a transparent affair, and the people who move in this area with great assurance must have some kind of mental connections that we normal people do not have.

In the case of Gauss, however, you can say that he was a lightning calculator; therefore he did it *that* way. I say he was a genius, a pure mathematician, and he did it *that* way. And who is true nobody will ever know. What is at stake and what I'm going to discuss today will be the connection between the two. But, before we do that, I have to make two preliminary but necessary distinctions. The first one I take from Lévi-Strauss, who somewhere (I don't remember where, but you will remember) makes a distinction between the engineer and the *bricoleur*. I think it is in the *La Pensée Sauvage*. The engineer and the *bricoleur*, which I translate as the tinkerer,—and that's me, I'm the tinkerer, so I know. The engineer is the type who perfectly clearly defines his objective, solves the problems of construction, designs everything, then orders the material in units that can be put together according to a pre-fixed method. The *bricoleur* is one who goes into his back yard, and there are pieces and bits, and if it doesn't fit, then he just takes something else. If there is finally a door knob lacking but there is a water spout, then he will find some way of turning the water spout into a door knob. This is the type of the inventor. He doesn't work with prefabricated material; he takes things where they are, and he has absolutely no conscience when it comes to linking completely different things and seeing whether he can't turn one to the advantage of the other. And that's the *bricoleur*.

So we can say that the engineer is a man who has a certain skill that can rise to the level of genius, but this is the way he operates. The *bricoleur*, the tinkerer, is characterized by inventiveness and by a preference for short cuts which are much longer than doing the prefabricated stuff. But it saves him ordering something from Handy City, because he has something in his back yard which really doesn't fit, but to make it fit, that's the thing. And he is the one to whom the characteristic of usefulness applies far more than to the engineer. What he turns up with is usually useful, whereas the engineer makes nothing that is ever useful in the sense that it is unexpectedly useful; it is premeditatively, preconstructively useful. And this usefulness is again the criterion that Poincaré uses.

The second distinction I want to make comes out of a statement for which again I won't claim anything, namely, the question: how did the Egyptians and other primitive people, but especially the Egyptians, produce the exact right angles they made? There are various theories. As you know, there are quite a few ways of producing a right angle without knowing anything about geometry. The theory I read about, evidently based on the finding of long staves that were used, was that they used to put three staves together, one of three units, one of four units, and one of five units. If you put them together, you get of course a right angle.

The Greeks also dealt with the problem of the right angle and they came up with the Pythagorean theorem, where $c^2 = a^2 + b^2$. What is the difference between the Egyptians and the Greeks? The Egyptians knew how to do it, and the Greeks generalized it. Instead of going: 3, 4, 5, they had a general rule. And not only that; they proved the rule. So, in brief, we have here stages and we have limits to each stage. What is the limit for the Egyptians? The limit for the Egyptians is that they do not get, evidently, pure mathematics (if this is all they knew, and I think we don't have any evidence of anything beyond it.) They were extremely precise; they got the value of pi down to an amazing extent, actually farther than they really needed, and so they knew a good bit, but evidently they did not develop any pure mathematics. They did not generalize.

The Greeks generalized, and they too had a limit, and the limit can be seen right from this. Here we have a 3, a 4 and a 5, and that is the reason why, in Fermat's theorem, $n > 2$ is excluded. Because $3^2 + 4^2 = 5^2$. Why did the Greeks not go farther than the Pythagorean theorem? Because they ran into the problem that if $a = 1$ and $b = 1$ then they have trouble, because $1^2 + 1^2 = 2$ and therefore c is the square root of 2. And there is no rational number which, when multiplied by itself, gives you two. This is the block, and this is why you find in Plato the problem of enlarging an altar, where you deal not only with the square root of 2, but where you then get into the three-dimensional problem of it.

So how do you get beyond that in mathematics, beyond the square root of two? You can get beyond it only if you push beyond the limits of the kind of mathematics that the Greeks had. And this great push began of course after the seventeenth century. There begins the great extension of the domain of numbers. There begins the problem of the so-called infinite in mathematics—what it is and what it is not. And then we got a great change around the time of Gauss and, after him, the beginning of the discovery of non-Euclidean geometries, and that brings us now to the creative act according to Poincaré.

I have used the first book edition of it in *Science et méthode*. The original essay, which is called "Mathematical Discovery",[10] was published as a result of a survey by a journal in applied mathematics that asked the mathematicians in France to answer a thirty-question questionnaire on every possible factor that may have had to do with creative work. There were a lot of silly ones. Two years later they added two more questions, and one of them had a considerable effect. They asked the question: have you ever found the solution of a difficult problem in a dream?

So let me very briefly tell you about one incident that illuminates very well how deep such questions go when they seem to be very silly. In working on my Cartesian bibliography I went through all the journals that were available to me from 1800 to 1960, among them of course the French philosophical ones. In one of them, 1945 or '46, I found an article—I think it was in the *Revue de métaphysique*—by the French mathematician Paul Lévy who taught at the Polytechnic Institute, on the question whether mathematicians can find the solution of a problem in a dream. The article states that he, Lévy, is absolutely and unshakably convinced that it is not possible. However, as an honest scholar he had to confess that it has happened to him. He says that he doesn't believe that this is how he found the solution but in all honesty he has to describe it. He was working, very typically, on a difficult problem, I believe a number theory, and then came

---

10. Henri Poincaré, "L'Invention mathématique," *Science et méthode* (Paris: Ernest Flammarion, 1908) 43–63; Eng. tr. by Francis Maitland, "Mathematical Discovery," *Science and Method* (New York: Dover Publications, 1952).

exam time and he had to lay it all aside. He had to grade papers and doctoral exams, and so forth. And then he had a dream, and in this dream he had suddenly the solution. He wrote it down the next day and went on with his exams, and afterwards he worked it out and found that it holds.

Now this is interesting, but I wouldn't have mentioned it if there were not a postscript. The postscript in small print says in effect: Monsieur Xavier-Léon [the editor of the journal] sent me the proofs of this paper, which I read with total unbelief. I have no recollection of ever having written it, and I certainly have no recollection of ever having had that dream. I told him so and he said that I had submitted this paper before the war, in 1939, and because of the war it had been impossible to publish it [Xavier-Léon was Jewish and ended in a concentration camp], but now that the war was over and the Germans out, he was taking the first opportunity to publish it, and here were the proofs. If you don't believe it, he said, here is the manuscript. Paul Lévy goes on: I looked at the manuscript. It was in my handwriting, and the signature was my signature, and I cannot deny any more that I wrote the paper. However, it does not in the least shake my conviction that this is totally impossible, and that a mathematician cannot solve a problem in a dream.

Now you see that you are touching on very deep layers, and what it comes to is of course the relationship between consciousness and the so-called unconscious in the creative act. A great deal has been written about that, and I would like to say, just as a preliminary comment, that when we talk about the unconscious we must not talk about an "it". It is not a something that you can locate. I don't know what it is. I treat the unconscious the way I treat stories like the egg of Columbus and the story of little Gauss, as a symbolism, a symbolism which is extremely useful because it tells us the truth about something which we cannot get hold of in its so-called natural state. And this is where I think that one day the connection between this type of creativity studies and the studies of the nervous system and the brain will link up somewhere, and at the end of this I hope I can give a few suggestions on that.

Poincaré wrote the paper which is the basis really of the excellent book I mentioned last week, Jacques Hadamard's *The Psychology of Invention in the Mathematical Field*, but I think the original is far more potent. Hadamard is useful because he brings so many other things together. He reads Poincaré for the explanation that he gives of mathematical invention. I read him simply as a superb observer of his own processes and as a great document of what the creative act is in reality. What he says about the interpretation I don't ignore, but I set it totally aside, because a man can be quite right about what he observes and quite wrong about what he interprets out of it. He can also of course be very right in what he interprets out of it although he is quite wrong about what was there in the first place. So we have to be a bit careful.

He asks first of all: what is mathematics, pure mathematics? It is not a logical work, a logical combination of all that mathematicians have known. There is, he says, an infinity of combinations of mathematical theorems, of bits and pieces, and most of them are useless. And so the work of the mathematician, the pure creative mathematician, is a work of choice. How does he choose? The criterion Poincaré gives is usefulness, both material usefulness and moral usefulness. Very interesting! He wrote that around 1905 and published it in 1906. And I quote, "Useful is what makes men better." This is supposed to be the criterion by which mathematicians choose between the various combinations they could make.

He gives only one example of what happened to him normally in tackling difficult problems. One of the greatest defects of this chapter is that he gives only this one example, which is very detailed. I am going to follow it all the way through. But I would like to have known a lot more—he hints that he had experiences of that kind in different ways and at different times. But we are going to take the one classical one, the way he invented or found the so-called Fuchsian functions, functions that he named in honor of the German mathematician Klaus Fuchs, whom he greatly admired.

I have broken this long account down into steps, and I want to begin with his own introduction to that account, where he says that what matters in mathematical invention is choosing, picking out from this mass of possibilities that which reveals relationships between hitherto seemingly unrelated material, preferably from widely separated fields or areas. And I'd like to say that this is, on the part of a mathematician (the highest and purest, the royal science), a statement that justifies interdisciplinary studies. He says that you don't get anywhere near where you want to be when you stay within your field. He is saying that the relationships to be discovered transcend this narrow division into fields. But how do you pick the fertile ones from the barren ones, from the enormous mass of the barren ones? How did he find this type of function? Let me begin with a quotation from Poincaré which Hadamard picked as the foreword to his own essay. "I would say that I have found the proof of this theorem in these circumstances. The theorem itself will have a barbaric name which many of you will not know, but that doesn't matter. What is interesting for the psychologist is not the theorem; it's the circumstances." And so, if I put my foot into it with the Fuchsian functions, I hope I will be excused. But I will be giving you the circumstances in the detail that Poincaré gives.

It begins with fourteen days where he tries to prove that there are no such functions as those he will later call the Fuchsian functions. He has an idea, he pursues it with everything he has, and he finds it doesn't work. He cannot prove that there are none. Now, of course it is always easier to prove that something is than to prove that it is not. That's evident. So the search begins with failure, but it also begins already with a notion that there is something of which he wants to prove that it cannot exist. So you find already at the beginning this unacknowledged and unconscious dichotomy between what he's really after and what he consciously tried to do. You will find that again in the case of Descartes, in the case of Rousseau, and in a number of cases.

Event number two: one evening he has a cup of black coffee, and he is not used to it, and that night he has a storm of ideas that clash with one another all night—I think many of us have experienced that, even without the cup of coffee—until two of them get together to form a stable combination. He doesn't make anything of it, but this is the clue to the working of the subconscious, as we shall see.

Event number three: the next morning he wakes up with the unshakable conviction that the functions that he wanted to disprove do exist, and also the notion that they form a class derived from the hypo-geometric series, that is to say, from one of the non-Euclidian geometry series.

Four: a few hours of conscious work later he has formulated the results of what happened in that night of the black coffee. Then he goes on from there, as he must, tries to represent these functions as a quotient between two series. And this he does completely consciously and with an exact aim—the engineering part of it. He is trying now to engineer a formula. He tries to establish the properties of the series, if they were indeed existent, and he finds out what these functions must do if they exist. The result: he has found what he later calls the Theta Fuchsian functions.

Now comes another typical event. A break. He gets an invitation to leave Caen, where he lives, to go on a geological excursion. He leaves his mathematics behind; forgets it all. They take the train to Coutances, where a bus is waiting. And here begins the usual account of how these things were found. I found it in about eight books already. He puts his foot on the first step of the bus and then he knows. And that is about all they tell you. At the moment he sets his foot on that step, the idea comes suddenly, unexpectedly, unprepared for by any previous thought. "I realized that the transformations I had used to define the Fuchsian functions were identical with those of non-Euclidian geometry." And then the next step. Having had this fulgerant illumination, he gets on to the bus and continues his discussion of geology with the others.

Rilke has written down the first line of the *Elegies*. He puts it in his pocket and goes on to write his business letter in his mind. I say this because I'm always accused of inventing things—which I do sometimes, but I invent on the basis of a lot of material. Well, you see the same thing happening here, there, and there. And this is typical: the continuation of the conversation, without pursuing the thought, and yet with the feeling of total certitude. Then Poincaré comes back home. "Returned to Caen, I verified the result that I had in mind." Why? A wonderful phrase: "for the sake of my conscience." I didn't want to make a fool of myself, you know, and so I verified it, although I was sure it worked. Then he thinks he is through, and he turns away to something entirely different, namely, to arithmetic problems wholly unconnected with the preceding, and he can't find any interesting results.

Next thing. Another break. He takes a vacation. He goes down to the ocean, thinking of quite different things. And then, a few days later: "Walking on top of the cliff, I had the idea, again with the characteristics of brevity, suddenness, and immediate certitude, that the arithmetic transformations of certain indefinite forms [that he had been working on before and that had nothing to do with the rest] were identical with those of non-Euclidian geometry." Now back to reflective, conscious thought. "Back in Caen, I reflected on the result; I drew the consequences, etc., and found that there are still other groups of such Fuchsian functions than the hypo-geometric ones . . ." the only ones that he had until then known. And what comes now is the discovery that what he has found is a whole domain, not just one thing, but a whole domain, the generalization, and again with this immediate certitude.

Now comes the next step, eleven: conscious work, attempt to formulate all of the things that he has found, one by one. And there is one that resists. This is crucial, because, he says, if this one falls, then the rest of them fall into place. It is the one big obstacle. "Yet all my efforts merely made me at first understand the difficulty better." All this work was perfectly conscious.

And now comes another break. He has to go and do his military duty at Mont Valérien, dons the uniform, and mathematics is off for the time being. "One day, crossing the boulevard of the town, the solution to the difficulty appeared to me at once." You may remember that in the first lecture I said that, if there are instances of this sudden illumination, they would be such that people would not only remember them, but would tell you exactly where they happened, when, at what time, and under what circumstances. Note: "as I was walking on the cliff," "as I was putting my foot down." And now we have "as I was crossing the boulevard." It is always this precise knowledge. "I did not try to work it out immediately, and only after my return to Caen, after my military duty, did I take the question up again. I had all the elements; I needed only to bring them together and put them in order, and I wrote the final paper in one go and without any trouble." And that is the account.

What you see is that it is not just the business of his getting on the bus and finding the solution to the problem. It is a rhythmical back-and-forth, a rhythmical change between conscious and unconscious thought, between relaxation and hard intellectual work. And now comes the theory. His theory is that there are four stages: the preparation, incubation, illumination, and then finally the conscious working out. And I would like to make two comments on that.

First of all, the sudden illumination. The word has been traced back to Graham Wallas, *The Art of Thought*

1926.[11] Actually it is already in Poincaré; it is already before Poincaré in Théodule Ribot, the French psychologist, *The Psychology of Attention*, 1889.[12] You can find it already, as I will show you, in St. Anselm. The illumination, that is to say, the enlightenment, the light, is the symbolism of the creative act. So it is not accidental that the word "illumination" appears in all of these accounts. The word "incubation", unfortunately, is to be traced back to Wallas. I say "unfortunately" because it gives you the impression that what happens before the illumination is that a hen is sitting on an egg in which something happens—an incubation. It is not like that, definitely not.

What is at stake is precisely the role of the so-called unconscious in that pause between the conscious work of preparation and the conscious work of drawing consciously the conclusions and writing the definitive paper. In between there is a gap that begins with a break. Sometimes the fellow is too tired. It is as if the brain had to be knocked out for these things to happen. In the case of St. Anselm he is so worn out that he cannot even sleep any more. In other cases, he is invited to go on a trip, and one begins to ask, with Freud, whether he was invited to go on the trip or whether he wanted to be going off somewhere where he couldn't think about it any more. But that definitely is the beginning of it. And the end of it is the fulgerant illumination, which is exactly described in all cases.

So what is the function of the unconscious? What is the unconscious as such? There is a very interesting clue which just shows you the difference between a self-observer of the rank of Poincaré and a very nice, intelligent, and sensitive scholar like Graham Wallas. Poincaré does not talk about incubation; he sees something, and what he sees is a wall on which there are fixed, he says, something like Epicurean hooked atoms. The notion is that the atoms have different shapes, they have little hooks. Some of them have big hooks and hook up with others, and other are more round, so that the fluid is the round ones. And when they begin to interlock, solid things begin to form. And, he says, I saw something like a wall where they were pinned on, and then suddenly a few, several of them, got loose, and began sort

11. Graham Wallas, *The Art of Thought* (New York: Harcourt, Brace and Company, 1926).

12. Th. Ribot, *La Psychologie de l'attention* (Paris: Félix Alcan, 1889).

of to dance around. (We'll get into the dancing, the dancing atoms, again in the case of the physicist Kekulé, who saw the dancing snakes.)

What you have again is this movement. Something that was solid begins to move. They start moving. Which ones? The ones that turn out to be useful. And he has a hell of a time telling us why the subconscious, which doesn't have judgement, picks the useful ones. I'm not going into that because in that case I don't think he took the break when he should have taken it. I would rather say what the upshot of this is, namely, the proof that they are useful, and here I can quote him verbatim. "The proof is the feeling of mathematical beauty, the harmony of numbers and forms, and the geometric elegance." So we are not talking about how men can be better than they are; we are not talking about the application; we are talking about beauty. He says this harmony makes it possible to have simultaneously the whole and all details as well before your mind.

Here I would like to make a reference to a very strange and debated document, a letter supposedly by Mozart, where he describes how he composes. The extraordinary thing is that he says: when I have the theme, the ideas begin to link up, and in the end I hear the whole composition, no matter how long it is, as a whole and in all its detail simultaneously. Now, if you think of a composer who has the whole of *Figaro*, or any other opera, in his head simultaneously, with every bar, it is unthinkable. But here we have something similar. The whole and all the details are clearly before the unconscious mind. Unfortunately the letter of Mozart is considered unauthentic. I don't know, it reads authentic, but . . .

In his interpretation Poincaré thinks that there are two basic differences between the unconscious and the conscious. The conscious is limited; the unconscious is not. Secondly, the unconscious, unlike the conscious, does not calculate things out. And now comes a wonderful description of the unconscious. Instead, there reigns in it "the simple absence of discipline, the presence of the disorder that stems from the accidental," in other words, complete freedom. Freedom is the simple absence of any discipline, and the presence of the disorder that stems from the accidental. I remember that Becket says something very similar at the end of his first novel *Murphy*. Remember? Murphy has tied himself naked to his rocking chair and is rocking, and he has a little gadget, a little gas stove, and he has turned it on, and he is waiting for the explosion, and the explosion produces chaos, beautiful chaos. You know the history of the word *chaos*, which becomes *gas*, so gas and chaos are the same thing. The beauty of it is the total disorder, because there is no more discipline, nothing fits anymore, everything blows around, and that is release. This is the end. So that is what Poincaré sees in the unconscious.

And now I want to give my own view of what really happens in this unconscious. I don't like to make predictions, but here I will make a guarded prediction. What I am going to develop here very briefly is based on a great many of these cases, every one of which I have studied in detail. I don't accept anything in a book; I go to the original and I try to find out as much as I possibly can. And I am convinced that one of these days neurology will come to results which in general support this interpretation. What makes me think so is that, after all, we have talked now twice about the relation between man's physiological constitution and the mental acts of creativity, and I've said very clearly that you cannot derive an understanding of creativity from these physiological mechanisms, but at the same time we can't have this, that or anything else unless we have the physiological foundation for it. It is just like saying that nobody can run the mile in four minutes or less unless he has two working legs. It's simply a condition. I therefore believe that it is in this area that we must look for an eventual coming together of two entirely different approaches.

Now, what are the conclusions? This unconscious process evidently—and Poincaré suggests it—runs parallel with and independent of the conscious working of the mind. It runs parallel with it and is independent of it. And it is so independent that the conscious mind doesn't know what is going on in the unconscious mind. He doesn't say anything about the reverse. Does the unconscious mind know what is going on in the conscious mind? Well, there is a hint. He says the unconscious mind doesn't work logically. Here the accidental reigns, and yet it is not just the accidental because there is choice. But it is certain that the freedom is in the unconscious and not in the conscious. There is not the discipline of the conscious; there is not the accustomed order; there is no compulsion.

What, then, happens there? It is at this point that we have to remember something that plays a very cardinal role here: the unconscious memory. In the Indian Mahayana philosophies there is a very extended analysis, you could say a phenomenology, of consciousness, with stages and levels of it. And the eighth of these levels is called the storehouse memory, a very high level of memory. Now, the storehouse memory of the unconscious evidently receives what is put in. It receives it not in the way in which a computer is programmed, because there are no instructions about how to use it. But it receives none the less, and what it receives are the results of the preparatory work and of everything that went before it. In other words, in this huge storeroom whatever is operative can walk around like the *bricoleur* in his yard, looking at things and moving them around, trying out, not systematically. And we have now the problem that really floored Poincaré: how is it possible to pick out from all the combinations of all that is possible, of which most is junk, the very few that are fertile? He doesn't realize that he had the clue in his hand and then gave it away, namely, the beauty of it. He calls it the beauty of it, but he also had another image that tells you what happens. It is like a constant shuffling and reshuffling of what goes on down in the unconscious. And he speaks of this linking up of two elements that form a stable combination.

Let me introduce an image of my own that you are all familiar with, and that is the image of a jigsaw puzzle. Imagine a jigsaw puzzle where you don't have the cover of the box to tell you what it ought to look like, and it is not one where you can say that everything that is blue goes on that side because it is either sky or ocean, but it is something abstract; it can be anywhere. Now we can imagine that the unconscious mind begins to put things together, and what sticks from the preparatory work is not the results but the failures. Somewhere there must be something in us, a memory that registers our failures. Because every failure is something permanent. Solutions are not permanent. Solutions can look absolutely right, you can even have the absolute conviction of certitude, and then they prove wrong. But failures are the blocks, you see, and these blocks are here and there and everywhere. And now the subconscious mind begins to put together the stable combinations, some here, some there. And then comes another phase of conscious work. Some preliminary results have been obtained, and then again a block comes, and that goes down, and eventually there comes then the point where everything moves together and there are only blanks left. And then these blanks will be filled by the work of the conscious mind, which doesn't know it is filling in the blanks. And when the whole thing is there, then comes that feeling of certitude that is not justified by anything that the conscious mind knows. Why? Because now there are no more contradictions. That is the moment which now presses for the fulgerant illumination. And why can it not be gradual? Because it has to be a breakthrough. Because the conscious mind is not prepared for it. The conscious mind may have been fighting for it; it may have believed it impossible; it may have gone off in an entirely different direction.

In the case of Kekulé, the great German chemist who was the founder of organic chemistry, this is a very well-known story. He had two great inventions or discoveries: one the structure of the carbon chemical compounds and the other concerning the way in which the molecule is formed. Both of them occurred in a similar way. He was riding a bus in one case and he saw the snakes dancing, and suddenly he realized that this dance was really what the structure is like. And then the other one, where he tried to write down the formula, and he couldn't and he couldn't because there was no way. It was a line from which you had to see each of the atoms, and it didn't fit. Again he was at that time sitting in a half trance and half sleep, daydreaming, in his chair by his desk, and he began to see the snakes dance, and one snake eventually bit itself in the tail. This is of course the old symbol of the *uroboros*, the snake that bites his own tail, the eternity symbol of the Greeks. Jung has a whole chapter on the *uroboros*, with all the mythology. The Aristotelian perfect form, the circle, because the movement goes on eternally. Kekulé sees that and suddenly he realizes that when you bend that line and bring it together, then everything fits. But he had to be in a trance because the conscious mind would not admit it.

So we have not cleared up that part of it: the independence, the process which is a shuffling and reshuffling, a constant one. And if Poincaré says that it is impossible from the infinity of possible combinations to select the ones that work, he overlooked the possibility that the subconscious mind may work, but not like a computer that just runs through the mill until it hits the right thing and then signals it. Rather, it takes notice of the blocks and it takes notice of the possible stable combinations.

And then you bring them together, and if there is a block that prevents that, then that goes down and never appears again. Until there comes this feeling of order, the order attained. So that the criterion that appears everywhere in the work of mathematicians, also of physicists—I don't know enough about chemists—but in physics, if it's pretty, it's possible; if it's beautiful, it's true. The absolute conviction comes with the beauty of it, and the beauty is that of order. It is very interesting that mathematicians have not followed it out, not even Birkhoff, who did that marvelous work on the mathematics of the beautiful,[13] because they didn't think of the beautiful as the impact of order; they thought of the beautiful as something that has to do with mathematical form. But I think that the beautiful as a symbol of order is by far the profounder and the more fertile conception.

In other words, what emerges from the unconscious is a new order. Then comes the last part of the work; then the rational mind has to take over. And there we will find that, after this illumination, usually most of what was revealed was lost and has to be recovered. So we do not have a very simple process before us, but you can now see that we are at the root, in the heart, of this creative act, symbolized in the work of a mathematician who has it easier than others because he can tell you very precisely where his obstacles were, what exactly happened.

So now questions.

A question from Hendrikus Boers, Professor of New Testament: What I don't quite accept is your explanation that it is at the moment where there are no further contradictions that the pause comes, for the following reason. I have a suspicion that your examples are only a selection in which it happens to work that way. In the first place it is interesting that the *bricoleur* form of the Egyptians preceded the Greek form that resolved it mathematically. What puzzles me is why it can then be explained, mathematically or in some other way. I suspect that only those cases where it is subsequently possible to give an explanation come to our attention, because that's the way we work, logically and mathematically, but I would not be surprised if those insights also come in instances that cannot subsequently be explained rationally or mathematically.

13. George David Birkhoff, *Aesthetic Measure* (Cambridge, Mass.: Harvard University Press, 1933).

Yes, of course, and you can also say that it is not true that it happens in every case, and that there are mathematicians who never had . . . etc., etc. But the case of Paul Lévy is very interesting: that it can happen to people who tell you that it can't happen. What's more, I don't see why a humanist cannot have the advantage that every scientist claims. When a scientist wants to find out something and the thing that he can use is a rat, he uses a rat, and nobody says: why don't you use an eagle? Maybe the eagle is different, but if it works with the rat then you can go on from there. In other words, we had the argument last week: why everything from the seventeenth century? Why the romanticism? Well, there is one very good reason: because these people talk. We don't know what went on in the mind of Pythagoras or any one of the great Greek mathematicians and scientists. Think simply of a sequence of three great men: Alexander, Julius Caesar, Napoleon. What do we know of Alexander? We know where he went and what he did, and the rest of legend. Julius Caesar? We've got a whole book on his conquests of Gallia, of France, and we've got a lot of very interesting anecdotes. For example, he was the first man—the Romans admired him for that—who could read a dispatch and keep on talking to others. In other words he didn't read aloud. It was considered something fantastic. [Laughter] No, no, this is very serious. The Greeks, the Romans, had to read aloud, and in the Middle Ages they still read aloud. They would have admired school children, grade-school children, here because they can read like this, and they know what they have read. So the connection between the audio and the visual was broken at some time.

And then you have Napoleon. On Napoleon we have books and books and books, and I'll give you an example of what treasures you find there. Someone asked him, when he was emperor, how do you operate? Every moment people come with questions. There is a military question, there is a question what should we do with this guy there who did that and that, and we have no money for this and that, and you immediately give an answer which is fully informed. You can't carry all that in your head simultaneously. Napoleon said: of course not, I have drawers in my head, and when information comes in, it falls into these drawers. (Like the Hollerith machine, you know.) A question comes, I pull a drawer out, I get the information out, and I give the answer. At night, he said, I shut all the drawers, and I am asleep. You see, you don't have that for Julius Caesar; you don't have it for the Egyptians. We have to fall back on the people who can talk to us and whom we understand.

None the less it is of course true that there are other ways of creativity. There are the people who are parked in madhouses but who are actually nothing but creative—this is something that has been occasionally advanced as a hypothesis—who never get to bring one order into focus and then stay with it. If you imagine somebody in whom these processes go on all the time, he is dysfunctional, just like animals that are wounded and run around in circles and can't move any more. So we have normal and we have abnormal things. I still don't know, for example, what happens in the mind of composers and in many other fields. But if you want to make progress there and want to be on a sure basis, then I personally find there is only one way: go to the sources, where somebody authentically described what happens, whether he does it in plain, overt language, as Poincaré does, or in symbolic language or in dreams or in whatever form, and investigate that. Then you have something that can be either proved or negated or modified. Then you have something in your hand.

Another question from the audience: It strikes me that the examples you have given are all from the range of mathematics, mathematical physics and theology. And it seems to me quite obvious that these are related one to another. Perhaps poetry and creative literature is prejudiced in the approach that people who do this tend to stress creativity as a kind of divine infusion, say. Therefore I think, and already have the suspicion, that memoirs of these people are prone to mystification about the facts. I never read about invention of this kind in philosophers, and there are biographies, there are self-documents of philosophers in all . . . But I haven't found it and I ask you, have you found similar statements of philosophers, how they come about their knowledge?

Yes, yes. The greatest document, which I am leaving for the last—so I can keep my audience, you know—is the dream of Descartes, on which I lectured in 1948 and in '54 and which is quoted in the literature, although I have not published it yet. He left us an account of three dreams in a row. But that procedure . . . yes, in Descartes you can prove it. I would also say that if you were to learn how to read philosophers differently, namely, not in the doctrinal way—he says so and so and then he proves and he argues—but if you would read them as I read poetry or literature or anything else, you would find all kind of hints. For example, I just had a discussion with Prof. Makkreel on the question of Kant on the sublime. Kant wants to do something with his philosophy; he has a scheme. Why does he want to do it? If you look a bit closer, you find that he is already on the way to a phenomenology of consciousness. It shows in his system as having *Verstand* at the bottom, then the higher form of understanding, *Vernunft,* and above that *das Schöne,* the beautiful, then the sublime or the highest, the *perihypsou* of Longinus. In other words, these are four levels of consciousness. They are disguised as methodology.

I could give you a little study that I recently made on verbiage in Hegel, where there is a sentence where the absence of one word proves that here something breaks through. And when you analyze that sentence, you find—it's in the very beginning of the preface to the *Phenomenology of Mind* (or *des Geistes*)—that it contains already all that he is going to say afterwards. So it is true, and in the first lecture in this series I investigated the way in which Rilke came to write the *Duino Elegies,* because here we have an account of how it happened and we have the result before us. So I would say in both cases: we have to acknowledge that creativity is a universal phenomenon; we have to acknowledge that it is as individually differentiated as all general phenomena are.

A question from Dr. Anibal Bueno, Professor of Philosophy at Morehouse College: I have a comment in relation to the Mozart letter that is apocryphal apparently. The American composer George Crumb has made exactly the same comment. He has made the same claim that he can have present in his mind some entire composition.

Well, I'll be glad if you let me have the reference.

Professor Thomas Flynn of the Philosophy Department: I find your discussion of the creative act very much parallel to what Michel Polanyi says in *Personal Knowledge.*[14] I am wonder-

---

14. Michael Polanyi, *Personal Knowledge* (London: Routledge & Kegan Paul, 1958).

ing what your comments on his position on the long term would
be. Certainly decisive, of course that's natural, from the same
quoting of examples. And also this notion of the issue burning at
the preconscious, subconscious level, forcing us with a kind of
urgency that can emerge so that the conscious is retrospective,
you know. Have you approached Polanyi in that manner?

Let me first of all make a personal statement. I have in part
deliberately left secondary literature or other explanations aside,
because I don't want to be mired in explanations. I want to get at
the original sources. And in the second place I find in a very
long life that I am a very slow developer. There are things that I
read as a boy and didn't understand until I was in my sixties. My
relation to philosophy began when I was a student, and every
student in a German or Austrian or Czech or any other Central
European university had to read Windelband's *Präludien*. I read
him and I thought that I had never read such gibberish. And I
said, never again. And I never did. I was told that Kant is an
impossible writer; so I didn't read him. Now I find that he is a
beautiful writer. But unless I have found something myself that
that man is talking about, the book is closed to me. And I don't
think I am the only one, except that I may be one of the few who
admit it. I don't think so.

So I can only say that I tried to study Polanyi's *Personal
Knowledge* and found it indigestible, because I evidently didn't
get on to what he is about. But I can tell you what he is not about.
All the analyses that I have made lead to the predominance of
the problem of order, which is an objective problem, if you will,
an ontological problem, order and disorder. I said in the first
lecture that we have this peculiar situation where, with the beginning of things, when things get in motion, order turns into
disorder, and the order that was before, that was the order of
chaos, of gas. Nothing moves any more, because everything is
alike. Now movement comes into it, and now we have a dynamic
which strives for order, and every order is a point of transition
for another order. I have today already announced another
thing that goes right into the literary problems: that in every
major work of creativity—I am not now speaking of mathematics
or of sciences, although about sciences I could say something—
certainly in the literary field and in the philosophical field you
have interlocking orders, and these orders have this in common:
in every case there is some point where they are not working

together. This is why in every investigation of creativity, where people talk about it (for example, in a symposium, about ten or fifteen years ago, of Jacques Monod), they see an oddity. Something sticks out where it shouldn't. If you grab it here, then you begin to distinguish between these orders. So we have a very complex thing before us. I don't see this kind of study of the complexity of it and of the order in Polanyi. If I had seen any of this, I would have read it all. But that, I think, is the difference. I'm not concerned with what happens in the individual. The problem of creativity is such that, wherever you grab it, you are in a general understanding of the world as it is, as it becomes and goes out of becoming. That means that we are all part of the great order and we are trying to understand as much of it as we can. And one way of it is this constant developing of orders. And there I come to inspiration; in addition to the light symbolism in creativity we have that other symbolism, divine enthusiasm, the recognition that this does not come from me at all. There are two proofs that we are not dealing just with psychological factors.

A question from Dr. Falkowitz: What criteria do you use to decide which accounts of how the mind works are reliable or accurate or useful?

Well, I can't say that I use criteria. What I do is try to do what every scholar in this case does. I have this text and I read everything I can find about Poincaré. I read the things that he has written, that have been checked out. I read his correspondence, where he talks freely, not in a formal way.

Follow up by Dr. Falkowitz: I guess my question is: how do you know that Poincaré has not perhaps entirely misunderstood just what it was that was going on in his mind?

Ah yes, there I use the simple criterion of consistency. That's what everybody uses, you know. Where his account is inconsistent, I know that he is in trouble. This is what I was talking about, where the two orders don't fit. For example, when he tells us that the mathematician makes his choice by the useful, and the useful is what makes men better, and then in the end he says it is that which is beautiful, these are two different things. So I know, not that he is lying, but that there is something unclear that he wants to say. And then you have to try and find out what he did want to say. And the final criterion is again the proof from the work that emerged. So that in the case of Anselm, where we have an autobiographic account, which has never been taken seriously because it has nothing to do with the argument, and follow it through the whole life of the man and the biography and his letters and his poetry, I can then show you what sense the argument makes when you take his autobiographical things into account. Now, if the autobiographical things were faked, this would not be the case. And there we have a final actual criterion, the case of language. Language is not a means of communication only, and unless you understand that you cannot use language as a criterion. If anybody has studied language as an expressive means, the way you study art, then a change in the language tells you what's going on in the mind, because the language comes out of the conscious mind in as much as it guides it, but the form it takes comes out of what's going on behind it. Freud has made that a principle when he talks about puns and jokes, you know, where you give yourself away.

Lecture Six

Order, Complexity, Intensity:
Toward a Theory of the Great Work

Today I want to talk about the work of art, especially the
great work of art as a paradigm. I will essentially give you a
paper which I gave on February 14, 1959, before the Georgia
Philosophical Society, meeting at Emory. That was before I came
to Emory. I remember the session very well. The society was very
lively and argumentative, and at that session there was not only
Charlie Hartshorne, really the only living American meta-
physicist, but there was also Julius Ebbinghaus, the well known
German neo-Kantian, who was a visiting professor here, and
there were present a number of quite outstanding people, and
we had a great debate on my paper and on a second one on the
same subject.

I would like to lead into this paper by talking about two
milestones or landmarks in the development of theories of art,
because at least the titles and the authors have helped produce
certain expectancies regarding any theory of the work of art.
One of these was Alexander Baumgarten, 1750, and the other is
Martin Heidegger, exactly two hundred years later, 1950, with
his very well known large-scale essay on the origin of the work of
art.[15] I am mentioning these because I'm not going to do either
the one or the other, but I have to explain why not and what it is
that Baumgarten has established, namely, the word "aesthetics"
and essentially the meaning of it, and what Martin Heidegger
has done at exactly the opposite end.

Let me start out with Baumgarten, whose concern in the
middle of the 18th century was the philosophical concern of the
18th century, not the problem of truth in any way but rather the

---

15. Martin Heidegger, "Der Ursprung der Kunst," *Holzwege* (Frankfurt a.M:
Vittorio Klostermann, 1950) 7–69.

problem of certain knowledge, epistemology. Now, what he wanted to know and find out was how to distinguish true knowledge from unreliable and false knowledge. And you begin, when you talk about knowledge, of course at the bottom, with the sense impressions which we receive of the world, and then going up—that's Baumgarten—until a certain level is reached where the highest area of knowledge is attained, the conceptual area. This area reaches up to the peak, which are the first principles from which everything else is supposed to follow. The art of distinguishing the true from the false then consists of examining what follows from these principles, the system, through a study of the rules, which are of course the rules of logic and those that emerge when you apply logic to the problem of conceptual truth. The man who does this examination is the philosopher.

There is nothing unusual about that, and the first volume of the two-volume work that Baumgarten published in 1750 called *Aesthetica*[16] is not remarkable at all. What made him a name that lasted was the second volume published in 1758, because in it he said that we still have to deal with another kind of knowledge which does not lead to intelligible concepts, does not lead to anything that will be amenable to the kind of critical judgement that also comes up from sense impressions and from what we learn about the world, and *that*, he said, although not higher knowledge, is knowledge too. This is the knowledge that we have of the world by way of feelings, or things that are pleasurable or painful, beautiful or ugly, and we form judgments about them too. They are not of the nature of the judgments up at the peak, because there is no truth claim. You can't say this is true or not. When you smell something, there is no question of truth. The only question is: is it this or is it that? None the less this too, he thought, must be amenable to some kind of logic of its own. This logic, which deals with what comes in through sense impressions, he called aesthetics, from the Greek word *aisthanein*, to feel, to preceive: what comes to us through perception.

Now, there is no such certainty about aesthetics as there is about metaphysics, about philosophy in general, because we are not dealing with abstract concepts that are anchored in whatever

---

16. Alexand. Gottlieb Baumgarten, *Aesthetica* (Frankfurt, Vol. I, 1750, Vol. II, 1758).

they are anchored in. It is not a question of truth claims, but there are rules none the less. And so Baumgarten deduced rules for the study of this area of knowledge. And just as he talked chiefly about the top area and the top of the top, in the so-called higher knowledge, so he also examined—and quite rightly—the top of this area where you don't have the infinite number and variety of sense perceptions but where you have something that corresponds to the abstract notions, concepts up here. And that is the work of art. And just as logic leads you through the maze of concepts, so aesthetics leads you through the maze of works of art, so that you can learn how to distinguish, to discriminate. It is not the philosopher who deals with this but the critic, whose name comes from the Greek word *krinein*, to sift through, to distinguish, to separate one from the other. In the English language the word "critic" has been retained for the fine arts and for literature. In German that would be called *Wissenschaft*, science. The German talks about *Literaturwissenschaft*, literary science; he talks about art science. Here the word "critic" is used and "criticism", art criticism, which doesn't mean that you criticize everything, but you learn to distinguish. That is typical Baumgarten language retained in this country. We are not going to have anything to do with that. I mention it only so that you can see where this notion of aesthetics started.

Two hundred years later, in 1950, you have Martin Heidegger, with an entirely different concept. For him the work of art gives us the highest knowledge we can have. It is not a propositional knowledge; it is not a knowledge where you say it is true that . . . ; it is not knowledge *about* anything. It is the knowledge of the truth itself, *aletheia*, which, in the much disputed etymology of the word, he translates as "unconcealment". What becomes unconcealed, what reveals itself in the "clearing", as he calls it, that is the work of art, is a manifestation of being itself. So you have again something which is not the ordinary truth claim but is in fact not a lower truth claim but an even higher one. In the work of art, being reveals itself as it is in the so-called clearing. We then get into a realm that is properly called ontology, the doctrine and study of being, being *per se*, being and existence, and that is the other pole. Somewhere between these poles is the area which I would like to enter. I would like to deal with the work of art according to this paper that I gave under the title of, I think, "Complexity, Order and Intensity". And I would like to give you very briefly one demonstration that will help us get through the first part, which is not the easiest because it is not very commonly done.

Let us assume that this blackboard is infinitely large and totally black; there is nothing on it. Obviously there is nothing you can say about it except that it's there. In this immensity we put one point. Now we can already say something. We can't say very much. It is not very complex, is it? Now we put just at random a second point anywhere, and what has happened? We now have two points, but we have also a relation between the two points, and suddenly the space that you have here has begun to look like something. There is a direction, and that direction is either this or it's that, but it could also be that or that, you know. We are suddenly faced with a multiplicity. Now, if you put a third point down anywhere, then you already get a balance or imbalance. So if with two and three points you can demonstrate a complexity that doesn't grow like 1, 2, 3, but like powers of those numbers—and very large powers—then you can understand how complex a work of art must be, even the simplest poem.

In order to link the theory of the work of art to the problem of creativity and creation, I would start out the way I started out at that time. (I published it later in the first *Festschrift* for Eric Voegelin on his sixtieth birthday.)[17] I talked first about the "thing-character" of the thing. I find now, upon rereading it—I hadn't looked at it for a very long time—that this is exactly how Martin Heidegger (whom I hadn't read at that time) begins: with the work of art as a thing, the thing-character. If you have read this wonderful and tremendously convincing work, you know that his great illustration is the pair of old, worn-out boots that van Gogh painted repeatedly. He goes then into the *Zeugcharakter*, the thing-character, of it, and how in the thing-character being itself reveals itself.

Now, every work of art is of course a thing. Whether it's the peculiar inverted comma that stands outside this hall—it's supposed to be a work of art—or whether it is a painting, whether it is a poem, a piece of music, or whatever it is, it is a thing. And if we want to understand it as a work of art of high and highest

---

17. Gregor Sebba, "Das Kunstwerk als Kosmion," *Politische Ordnung und Menschliche Existenz. Festgabe für Eric Voegelin zum 60. Geburtstag* (ed. Alois Dempf, Hannah Arendt and Friedrich Janosi; Munich: G. Beck, 1962) 525–540.

order, we must first look at it as a thing among things, because its character as a work of art stems from its thingness. Any and every thing is inexhaustible. It is the center of a field of possible statements about it.

I'll demonstrate that. Here is a thing, and here is another one. You can never exhaust the statements that can be made on either this or that. You think it's nothing, it's just a plastic spoon. But ask an Assyrian or a Babylonian about that! Ask somebody for whom this particular spoon meant something at a given time. You think about the spoon as it lies here, as you stir your coffee, and as it is used. You think about what it is made of, about its color. Every time you turn it, it looks different. In other words, it is the center of a field of statements which is, on principle, indefinite, perhaps infinite.

Not only that. Suppose I were to pick up a piece of rock. In fact, in my lecture in '59, I gave the example of a piece of rock which my landlord, Craig Orr, in Athens, Georgia, picked up, and we concluded eventually that it had been carved by an Indian. The rock has a history. Even if nothing is carved on it, it has a history. It wasn't always as it is. It must have come off something, and it will begin to weather. It will turn into all kinds of things.

So you have two fields in the thing. You have one field that is the field of internal complexity: anything that you can say, that you can read off this spoon. The other thing is, of course, the whole surrounding, encompassing—*umgreifend* is the word that Jaspers, the philosopher, uses—reality of which this is a part, in which it is embedded. Whose spoon was it? All this belongs in here: the culture that produced it, the design of it, and so forth. This is the external or temporal dimension of it. And so we have a complex structure, both internally and externally, and the two interlock, and I call this structure well ordered. The complexity of a thing, including the complexity of the work of art, is an order of orders. And it is totally futile to consider a work of art from the point of view of one order. For example, you have a lyrical poem. It has a rhythm; it has a word structure, a sound structure; and then it has the structure of meanings of each word, and each word is again a whole field, as you can see when you go through a dictionary.

What, then, is a work of art? What is this spoon? Because it too is a work of art. It wasn't born like that. It was made. And it has a shape, on which one of our faithful listeners here has written a whole book, on how you can from the shape of things deduct the attitude of those who made these things: their epistemology, their ontology, etc. He doesn't believe that he did it, but I know he did. It is Professor Scranton, who taught here until, I believe, 1961, and left much, much too early for all of us.

Eric Voegelin, the philosopher, has a word which I stole from him. He didn't use it in my sense but it fits. He calls such things a "cosmion". A cosmion of course is a little cosmos, and the word "cosmos" has two meanings. It means first a universe, and in the second place it means order. And because it is order it's also for the Greeks beautiful, and therefore we have the word "cosmetics". So we get from the universe to cosmetics in one go. A cosmion is a well ordered thing that has the character of the universe. It is well ordered, and it has beauty or whatever it may be; it has internal relationships. Any and every thing is a microcosmos, a cosmion, because everything that you find in the great universe is in some way reduced here to that one single little thing. That is the general notion that things participate in one another, that goes right back to the pre-Socratics, as you know.

So with the complexity we have already the concept of the order of orders, and as such we have a third notion that I cannot really translate. I use the German term *das Werkgesetz*, the law of the work, by which I don't mean a law that is imposed upon the work. That's how Baumgarten conceived of it. Baumgarten thought: just as there are logical rules for our concepts, so there are rules, there must be rules, for the work of art. And that is where the notion began that dominated the great period of the baroque and then the nineteenth century and way into the twentieth century: that, for example, every type of literature has its own set rules. They are not made by man, but they are in the thing itself. I'm not talking about that kind of rule. I'm speaking about the individual character of a work as being lawful. I will leave the discussion for later, because what you get into here is the difference between something that is, as we say, well ordered, organized, individual, and at the same time it is not supposed to be, or is not, accidental. The relationship between lawfulness and the accidental is of importance, but I'll talk about it later. You know perfectly well that if I were to take this spoon and mount it, for example, on a garbage can, I could put it into a museum, and it would be exhibited as an example of some kind of new art. Right? It is only when it is lying here that it's nothing. As soon as you take this and do something with it, its character has changed. And that is when you see that if it's this, it will have to have certain characteristics, which for the thing in its role as a work of art are immutable, relatively speaking. And yet it doesn't last; it changes. The best example is of course a work of art that is made of words. For example, we read Homer, we read the *Iliad*, and we have no idea what it sounded like. We reconstruct the meaning of words, but we can only reconstruct them on the basis of all that *we* know about words, and Homer had no idea of what we know. In other words, the words themselves change over time, and the words you use to speak about the work of art change. So there comes the question: what does time do to a thing that is supposed to be lawful in itself?

This leads now to the question that I'm raising, namely: is there something that is invariant in the work as regards time? It is the old question of interpretation that you can find in any serious work by somebody who knows what he is doing. You read in a real interpretation of Dante the first question: what do I interpret out of the work and what has been interpreted into it? Since you can't take yourself out of the work of interpretation—the interpreter can't disappear behind the work—there are always these two factors. And the question then remains: what is, for example, the *Divina Comedia* of Dante? You can only answer, it is that in the work which persists over time. And unfortunately it is not even the written letters that persist, or else we wouldn't have all those critical editions, where the editors disagree whether that word was in there or whether it was misspelled or what not.

So we are now introducing time as the factor that makes it impossible to define any work of art, makes it impossible to say what is called a definitive work of art. And so we have to come to the conclusion that the life of the work of art is in time. It is a continuous coming into existence and passing out of it, giving birth to untold simulacra, little images called interpretations. If, nonetheless, there is something that is invariant, persistent through time, then it must surely be that which makes the work what it is in the course of time. This must then be the engendering principle of the work, its DNA, so to speak.

We have had examples of that. The French poet Paul Valéry suddenly, as he was walking, heard a rhythm in his ear. It was a very marked rhythm, not the common French poetic rhythm that you all know. And he went around looking for a subject to pin this rhythm on, to write a poem on, something that had that rhythm. You have to write about *something*! That's one case. In Joyce, in *Finnegan's Wake*, what was the origin of that most complex work? It is simply the pun as the ultimate contrapuntal method, a counterpoint where all tunes are simultaneously playable, and played, which creates a field of meanings through which the work moves without going anywhere. All motion in that work is self-centered, circular, and therefore connected with every other motion. And then Joyce had to find something to apply it to. So everything, the myth, etc. comes later. There is a generative principle—and I could show you that in the case of *Faust*; I could show you that in the case of Eliot, where, by the way, it has been shown. That is what creates the law that governs not only the work but the genesis of the work.

A really good poem, a painting, or whatever it is, doesn't come into being by a creator sitting down and figuring out how he is going to do it. He's got to have a feel of what it is going to be, and that can be so vague that he himself doesn't know what to do. But that is what will produce the first shape, what will produce the first act, scene, or what, the nucleus from which the rest then develops. And as it develops, of course, it will change.

I have a number of questions about that. The first one: how is it possible for a creator, if you have this complexity, where you have so many aspects, as we call them . . . how can he keep all that in mind? It is not always as difficult as one thinks. Telemann, the German baroque composer, who was a contemporary of Bach, as you know, was once sitting drinking wine in Hamburg. They talked about the difficulty of writing a four-voice fugue (where the theme comes in four times), the difficulty being, of course, to find a theme that can be handled in the very intricate and precise sequence of the complex developmental form of the classical fugue. They said it would be impossible to sit down and write an eight-voice fugue, that is to say, one that is at least twice as difficult to do, without considering the whole development from beginning to end. Telemann, who was presumably already somewhat in his cups, said that there was no difficulty at all. One could very well invent a theme immediately and sit down and write it in proper form. So he sat down and wrote it.

Whether that is true or not I don't know. But it illustrates two things: first the complexity which any kind of formal work of art of a higher order requires, and secondly, the role that the craftsman may play in keeping all these different strands in mind simultaneously. However, we can be very sure that the fugue Telemann wrote down at that time—if he did write it down—is not one of the great masterpieces of music. That requires something more than what the Germans call *Kunstverstand*.

But this is not how these works really come into being. Because what really happens in the creative act is that the creator has established a field that has a center somewhere (an ill defined center but for him it sits somewhere) which now gives order to the process of bringing something into being. It is just like the genesis of a human being. You start out with two cells that join, and there is something in this cell and in that that governs the development, and only then come all the external and the internal complications and changes and so on. But at that moment basically a whole field is determined: this is going to be this and not that. Whether this will be here or there is a very different question. Goethe was right when he described the creative process as one where *die Fäden ungesehen fließen; ein Schlag tausend Verbindungen schlägt*—the great example that has been used again and again of the loom, of the weaver, where you throw the shuttle and the threads flow and you don't even see how. You throw the shuttle, and one throw will make a thousand connections, automatically. He doesn't have to say: now I'm going to do this and that, because that is all already in the origin of the work. And then comes the thing that makes these studies so interesting and so difficult: he throws it and it falls to the ground and it hasn't made the thousand connections!

In my living room there hangs a painting which those of you who gave me the pleasure of your presence may remember.[18] I got that painting because I was there when the painter did it and we were engaged in a talk about creativity. He was painting, and we were talking, and suddenly he said, "Oh my God, I've ruined it." He had put in a spot of very bright red. "It ruins the balance of the whole paining. What am I going to do?" I said "Scrape it off." He said, "I have never scraped anything off. I'll just throw it away." And then he turned around and said, "Now wait a

18. A gift to Gregor Sebba from Carl Holty.

minute! Wait a minute!" And suddenly there was a red here and a red here, and then came more of it, and the whole thing was restructured. Because he realized that, with this one mistake he had made, the balance had changed but the new balance was better. That happens all the time. But none the less, when it happens, once something is accepted instead of being thrown out, one of the possibilities will be followed out logically until another kind of balance emerges. But it has to be a balance. It if doesn't come out that way, then it *was* a mistake.

Rilke has an expression somewhere that is very telling.[19] It is taken from something he greatly admired, those very fine, especially Renaissance, line drawings of great masters. You know, they go very quickly, and they are very fresh. They are not preconceived; they are not tainted with too much thought. He just sets it down. Sometimes it happens, says Rilke, that the hastily snatched sheet of paper takes the line off the master's hand without his knowing, and this isn't the line he intended. And yet the line the paper captures is the *real* line. If it had been where he had wanted it, it would already have been a different and a wrong line. That is the poet speaking, who knows that a wrong word anywhere can be the true word and that what he thought would have to be the true word has to give way and maybe the poem has to change.

So we can, then, say what the law of the work is, the work's own law. It is its unmistakable essence, grasped as gestalt, with all its inherent and explorable possibilities, as Goethe put it, form that has been stamped as an individual form and is now organically developing. Only then, after that, comes the second phase of bringing a work of art into being, and there the German word is *Kunstverstand*, meaning knowledge, artistic knowledge, know-how, and of course also accident, even in the know-how. But basically we can say that a great work is never thought out beforehand from beginning to end. Something is incarnate in the work, and this is what makes it ultimately understandable; this is its unity. I call the fundamental concept of the incarnated law the style of the work, which is the term for its individual and its generic gestalt in the sense of gestalt theory.

From this analysis several important findings follow. First,

19. *Sonnets to Orpheus*, Second Part, II.

there should be a method of interpreting a work that allows us to separate out the interlocking orders, show their interconnection, and so reach the underlying law of the work, the gestalt. I developed this method and practiced it, when I was teaching at Emory, under the title of the climactic line method. It fastens on what we discussed before, on the oddity. When you have something that is very regular and you can't find anything that is odd, then you don't have to worry about interpretation. It will be very easy because it isn't going very deep. But in any very deep work you will find something that is not as it should be. And it takes some peculiar sense which today, when it is becoming rare evidently, is very highly prized among scientists, for example: the ability to see what shouldn't be there but is, the oddity.

What is that oddity? When you think of orders as a sort of cubic interlocking of things, then you will find that sometimes they interlock very smoothly but sometimes one sticks out a little bit, and then you get a word that sounds different from what it should be or an idea that doesn't fit. It is something that puzzles you, and you think: there is a mistake here. That may be, and probably is, the one word, the one place, the one line, that raises the question that will open up the law of the work. I have tried it with many students and I have found that there are two student types. The ones who are the systematic minds, the precise ones and the good learners, will never see the oddity. They come with a great collection of oddities but these all explain themselves. And then there are people who are like dogs. They sniff, and they will definitely sniff where there has been another dog before. That is the oddity. There is no way in which you can teach that; that's what I found. It is the gestalt that breaks through the orderly structures to make a rough edge.

Now we have still the last and the biggest question before us. We have talked ultimately about the work of art as a thing, and its structure, but we have said nothing about what separates it off from other things, and that is an important question. You can go to any beach and you will see a lot of driftwood. You take one home and it's no longer a piece of driftwood; it's a work of art. And you know that anything and everything can, even if it is only for a moment, become a work of art as you look at it. I don't think there's anybody of any perception or depth who has not had this experience. You look at something totally familiar, that clock, for example, and suddenly for one fleeting moment there is more there than there is. That is an experience that I think everybody has had.

What is it? This is what I mean by intensity. Intensity is what brings the perceiver, the contemplator, into the configuration of the work. We have talked about the work, about the structure, about accident, about time, but we have never said anything about those to whom it is addressed, and that includes, of course, first of all, the creator. Normally you can look at any work of art simply as a thing, but as a work of art it is not *intermediately* experienced. When I show you this spoon, there is no contact between you and the spoon. It is just a spoon; you know what it is, etc., etc. There always a mediation, a concept. You know what the spoon is for, how it comes here, etc. Not so with the work of art. The work of art has an immediate impact. And this impact is an act of identification that reaches down to the very ground of the self.

This is not true of every work of art. (I'm anticipating the main objection.) There are lots of works of art that are not of that kind because there are lots of works that are not at the top here. There are in fact very few works that are at the top. Among them are some very small things, and we should not simply judge all of these by one standard. But the work of art that maintains itself through time certainly has the character of this impact, this confrontation. And if you ask: why does it make this impact, why is there this peculiar exciting and worrisome identification, then, going back to our previous analysis, we find it to be a confrontation between what I call the given order and the well ordered order of the cosmion. The given order is the order in which we are born and that grows up with us. And that order is different from the order we find in the work of art, without analyzing it. The work of art, in other words, is a new experience in a very different sense from normal new experiences. When I speak of identification, of the ground of self, etc., I do not mean anything like being swept off one's feet, "*Erhebung* without motion," to quote Eliot. It is simply an analytical statement of the specific kind of impact of the work of art or any other encounter of a high order, like a line, a word spoken or read, or a thought, an event, as a revelation of a hitherto unsuspected order. Not every work has this kind of impact at all times. It has happened—again, I think, to all of us—that, reading some text that we know by heart, suddenly something strikes us. We know it by heart and yet it is suddenly new. That is what I am talking about.

In our regular world, the world in which we live, we are familiar with things as they are and there is a place for them and we know the order of things. It's not a very good order. There are contradictions; there are unresolved situations, impasses, but it doesn't normally bother us. If it bothers somebody too much, we think that person is sick. Why doesn't it bother us that we are in a world that is not well ordered? Because we know our way around. For example, I see that object, and that's fine, but if I were to go around and see what's behind it, then I don't know, so I'd better be a little bit careful. In other words, we know our way around in our own world, and that enables us to live within an imperfect order and feel at home in it.

Compare that to the order of the work of art, and you get a very different situation. There the order dominates the work, and only the fact that it is still a human creation and therefore not perfect prevents this order from being absolutely perfect. In fact a work that was perfect would be almost unacceptable to us. But this order that is in there is part of the order of the work. If, for example, you get lost in *Faust II*, it's not because there is something wrong with the work but because this is a work that is very foreign to you, and you accept that. And with every poet, with every playwright, with every painting, you accept the presence of things that shouldn't be in there, but they are minute compared to the great contrasts in life, to the great discrepancies, to the great unresolved conflicts between order and order. And because this is the nature of this impact, therefore the impact does something to us. It does not do to us what some people say it should do. There are always moralists, and they think that the work of art should also be part of our moral life. Right now we live in the phase of American civilization where the big boys of the entertainment industry tell you that this is art, therefore you must like it, whether you do or not. That hasn't happened before, and I hope it won't happen again. But we have to recognize that even in a specific work that we know and that has a tremendous influence upon us there are those moments where the work is totally dark. We read it and it's boring; it says absolutely nothing. That can happen. It can also happen, as I said, that something that is not a work of art at all may have this impact. But one thing is certain. Where this impact occurs, it occurs because order is, so to speak, concentrated in something that we can grasp. We are not confronted with ourselves and the world and everything. We don't get lost, as we do when we try to make sense out of the world, when we ask ourselves seriously: why am I doing this really? What am I here for? The work of art, in other words, is concentrated order, and it does not have the kind of darknesses, labyrinths and 'hopeless impasses of the world as we know it. In the work of art we more or less move freely but always bound to what is in the work itself.

The formula for this kind of concentrated order is one that I also developed before I got to the test which has established the word. (I did not know it at the time; I was a professor of economics, after all.) This is the work of art as an epiphany of pure order in contrast to the unresolved and unresolvable order of our own personal world. What the work encompasses is merely a particle of the great reality, a selection, a small morsel, of the overwhelming abundance of being. But this little bit of world is ordered through and through, and its form endows the subject matter with the character of truth. It is not what it says, but said in this form it is endowed with the character of truth. This is the point where this interpretation of the work of art touches upon Heidegger. It is not what they have said, but if you read Eliot or Shakespeare or whatever you like, if you look at prehistoric art or whatever it may be, you will find that it has an order that has the quality of truth.

And now I come to the last area upon which this theory touches, into which it has to go. I already mentioned it when I said that the impact of the work goes to the ground of the self. And so in the end I have to speak about the self and about what the self is made of, not of its form, of its own law that is given, but as the self that grows, Goethe's *geprägte Form, die lebend sich entwickelt*, the form stamped on the material, which now organically develops. And that of course ties in with what comes up from here and goes into the work, and at the same time goes down because, if this is world, from which things come up, then the self has to go down via the work of art. The work of art is novel on principle. Why? It is just as novel as any child that is born. Every child is like every other child, except that there has never been one exactly like that. That is true of course of the work of art. From the creator's viewpoint it is a new ordering, a reordering, a remodeling of human experience. What is grasped is a new order of orders, which is as yet free of any ties to any specific content.

What is content? Content is of course not a statement of something. Works of art either make no statement whatever or, if they make a statement and you take it out of the work of art, it becomes so trivial that it is almost pitiful. If you want to know what I mean, then just look at the lovely condensations of plays on the television or the condensations of novels. Something is rotten in the state of Denmark. Prince Hamlet finds out what it is. He kills the evildoers and dies in the process. That's *Hamlet*. That's the statement. Makes no sense! I have conserved somewhere in my junk two pages from a *New York Times Magazine* of about thirty or forty years ago, listing the best plays and a brief statement of the thesis of each play. You read them and it's absolutely hilarious. Man is miserable; man is glorious; man is this; man is that. And you say: now, what for? This is nothing. And yet even a work that says nothing says something. That is the paradox of the work. And we have to take it seriously if a work which really literally says nothing has such an impact on somebody that he or she says: it has opened a whole world for me. This has to be taken literally, and I recall a phrase from Eliot: "a new world and the old world made explicit." This is the description of the impact. I could quote you other writers, other poets. I could quote you artists, painters, sculptors. I don't know about architects, because with architects you get into a different sphere. Architecture is basically a symbolic art and a socially symbolic art. But where we have the individual arts, there certainly this statement holds.

We can, then, call the creation of a great work of art an establishment. And what is established is a new type of human experience. It is not what it says; it is a new type of human experience. And this experience has now become incarnate, as form. It is well ordered as it enters into a life of its own. This life is its existence in history. What the work says does not change and does not remain the same. And yet the work does remain the same in as much as it is different from all other works and things. Even where there is change through time—and there is change through time everywhere—two different things change in time differently. They may merge. It may be that after a while, after a few centuries, you can't tell any more whether something is part of another work or whether it ever was a separate work.

That happens. It can be that it falls apart. But the core of it, that which comes through, through time, that which sets it off from all other works, that remains intact as a phenomenon of invariance within change, and with it a form of teaching the beholder or listener or reader, teaching him something that is new to him. For if a work represents a new experience, then that experience is not common to the others. And it may not even be common to the creator himself. We have testimony after testimony, of poets, writers, dramatists, etc., who say: when it was finished, I read it and I didn't understand it. He no longer sees it as it was when it came into being.

So the role of the creator is creative in the most literal sense. The creator gives life to something novel, and therefore there is the problem of understanding the work. But the work is not novel in the sense of being a creation *ex nihilo*, out of nothing. The great creator makes clear what is. He lets the structure of what is appear before us in its purity. And this structure of what is is what Heidegger talks about when he talks about the clearing in which the truth emerges, not the truth of something, but the truth of being, being *per se*. But he can do more than that. A creator can and does very often anticipate future orders of life that do not yet exist. And he can open up new realms of experience; he can make them accessible by creating a language for them. This language does not have to be a word language; it can be a language of forms. It can be a language of new material to be used. This is how civilizations come into being. They come out of something that is felt as a new "law of the work", which then finds expression in gestures, in myths, in buildings, in customs, in infinite ways that make it transmittable, and the culture lives as long as this transmission can go on. It is broken when that dies off or is destroyed. Even if there is nothing novel at all in the content and in the form, a great work of art founds an experience by giving it unique intensity.

Far more important still is the creator's role in bringing to premature life hitherto unheard-of experiences that remain inaccessible to his own generation. Rilke didn't understand the *Sonnets to Orpheus*, which he wrote in the wake of his *Duino Elegies*; he had to learn them. And the *Elegies* were ununderstandable. I remember in 1922, when the work came out, my friends and I immediately put together our pocket money—we were sixteen or seventeen at the time—and bought a copy, and then we sat there, and said: what the devil does he mean? Totally ununderstandable! You read about people who grew up when Eliot was at the height of his fame. They say the same thing. There is a line that says something to them they don't understand. The poet, the writer, even the architect, the painter, creates the ability to experience what has not been experienced before. The work carries this power, and what the work does is to enable others to have the experience vicariously, not originally but vicariously. In other words, you learn it just as the child learns reading and writing in school. This is why, for example, it is impossible to speak good German today without speaking the language of Goethe. You need only look at that wonderful volume by Fischer on Goethe's *Wortschatz*, the words that Goethe coined, that didn't exist before. You look at it and say: but that's a very common word. It was not; it was absolutely new in his time. What Goethe introduced into that language was a dynamic—words that are formed to have direction. I don't want to give you examples because it is not your own native language. But the same thing happens with every great poet. You have in English the greatest example of all, Shakespeare. Just look at a Shakespeare vocabulary.

Now, when people are confronted with something new, they do not usually leap in and try to absorb it. The idea that they ought to do so is a very peculiar novel modern invention. They try to stay away from it if they can. And that explains why some of the greatest works die on their feet, especially works of old age. Because you have to understand that old age is not an age of senility but of the highest powers. Somebody in his old age doesn't look at things the way you do; he looks past it, because he already has all that behind him. So, as he looks past it, he sees something that is as yet impossible to conceive by those to whom he addresses himself.

And so it happens that if you look at, for example, the standard German encyclopedia of the time of about 1770–90, twenty, thirty, forty years after the death of Johann Sebastian Bach, the time of Goethe, you will find a lot of Bachs. One of them is the old man, Johann Sebastian Bach, who was a very good organ player, a very capable teacher, who wrote a number of very dry works which are purely didactic and teach you how to use your fingers. You will also find that there was one man who grew up after Bach's death, born the year before Bach died, who recognized that music for what it was. That was Goethe, a kindred spirit. At the same time, when Goethe was well into his middle age and beyond, there was Beethoven, and Beethoven and Goethe met in Karlsbad, taking the waters, and Goethe's only comment was: he has no manners! So Goethe locked away his *Faust*, the second part. He said—with regret, because he would have loved to know what his intimate friends would say about it—I know that when this is published, they will demolish it; they will say it is a work of total senility, stupidity, and it may be a hundred years before it begins to be understood. That was very precise. It was almost a hundred years. You also have the example of Beethoven's own late quartets, which were considered unplayable after his death. And there's that wonderful quintet, the only quintet, the only chamber music, that Bruckner ever wrote, one of his most brilliant works, which is still not played, still not being listened to, because it doesn't fit. So you find that it takes time. Rilke was not understood until the interpreters came in. Some of them of course were very good; others were not, but they began to talk about it, and suddenly there were such concepts as the *Doppelbereich*, the double realm of life and death. The whole existential vocabulary of Rilke began to sink in, and with it these experiences.

It can take a very long time before that happens. Why? Because a great creator can anticipate things which in his time play no role but will in a future time become vital to society as a whole. The shock of two world wars that created existentialism, the existentialist wave, was anticipated, for example, by Franz Kafka, who died in 1924 and had by that time already ordered that all his works be destroyed because they were no good. Rilke had died in 1926. And you will find all these forerunners of existentialism who suddenly emerged. It turned out that Pascal was one of them, and Kierkegaard. Why did it take so long? Because in the Germany of Emperor William II there was no room for them, and in the empire of Queen Victoria there wasn't either, and even in France there wasn't. So gradually situations develop where man needs something to hold on to. And it is then that great works turn out to be great works. We should never write one off, and we should never say, as my students always said: it couldn't happen today that a writer like Kafka, a composer like Schubert, dies practically unknown. I used to say to them: tell me fify years from now. You have no idea who is going to emerge out of your own time, and I am willing to lay any bet that there will be one or two or three of whom we have never heard. It can happen and it does happen today. Created material is being destroyed today as it always has been. And if it weren't for the fact that there is so much of it coming, we wouldn't have the kind of tradition and history we have.

So we can say that the work of art is active. It changes, it educates, and it does so by going to the very roots of our existence. The presence of a higher order forces us either to yield and to change or to refuse to change. The inability to yield to the impact of any work of art bespeaks a limitation, perhaps to the point of weakness, a limitation in vitality. And yet to enter into the higher order of works of art is to become alienated from lower vital regions. The center of meaning shifts from the given to the formed. This claim to surrender some of that which is given for the sake of a higher order and a deeper experiencing implies a call for a decision concerning the meaning of one's own existence and life. In this sense the full experience of the work of art is an act that could be called a religious act, and I would call it that if the word weren't so murky and so hard to define. But it is more than an aesthetic one; it is definitely more. The decision is ultimately an existential one. The difference between life and lack of life, between life and death, is a gradual one. In the end it is not the duration but the intensity of life, the intensity and not the duration or the amount of experiencing, that matters. In the experiential intensity the self expresses itself. In learning higher orders, the self establishes itself in the precise sense; it sets itself off from all that is non-self. And so we might say that in learning the well ordered new worlds, we learn what we are and who we are. We learn it by ordering ourselves, our own selves, into an order that transcends the self. The experience as such is pure self, and that which is experienced is world, so that the work of art shapes not only perception, knowledge, but the very life of the self. In experiencing the work of art as a cosmion, the self experiences the well ordered world with all its tensions, its yearnings and its fulfillments. That is what the theory of art looks like to me when I look at the very top of it.

And now I shall answer the question which is on all of your minds: what about the work of art that is lower? I say, when you want to know something, start at the peak. And then you know that every step down will get you a bit further down until you are where you started from. But if you try not to start at the peak but to climb up, you will be exhausted before you get there. So if you want to talk about the work of art, don't start by talking about the small things, which are very easily explained. What needs to be explained is the greatness of it, which will take us back to the first lectures. I began by saying that there are two types of words in the problem of creativity: the *kri-*, or *kre-*, *creative* words, and the others, the words on the root of *skap*, or *skaf*, or *schaf*. The root of *schaffen* pertains to the making of something out of nothing; it also pertains to the incessant recreation and reproduction of what is there, including sex, etc., etc. The other root is *kre-*, "make". What I have presented here is the outline of a theory of the work of art which shows that it is not only the creator who makes things but the work of art itself. What it makes is us.

Thank you.

First Question: Today you have spoken about the teaching art offers for everybody. And that teaching is of something new, something hitherto unexperienced. But, if so, you must always have a counterfoil to see what is new against the old. I think this calls for the introduction of a more historical view of things made by other people. I think there is no possible introduction to art without canonics, without things as great holders of ideas existing in them, and without a measure of the distance of the new and latest art creation in relation to its predecessors.

I appreciate that very much. What you say is absolutely true. However, let me say this: if you encounter somebody, then either you know that person or you don't. There are cases where you're not sure: do I know the person or don't I? These are very disagreeable cases. But basically the new sets itself off from the old, and if it does not then there is no problem. I just reread a paper I wrote and published on Stefan George, on the hundredth anniversary of his birth, where I reviewed briefly a work which begins by taking this, I think, greatest German poet of his time, and comparing him with Geibel, Freiligrath, and that kind of poet.[20] What for? There is at every time a kind of standard

20. Gregor Sebba, "Das Ärgernis Stefan George," *Colloquia Germanica* (1970) 2/3, 202–231.

poetry, and if there is not, then you are in a period of flux, when the old examples don't hold anymore. But so long as they hold, there is always a standard. That is not the problem. The problem is when something enters that's not in the standard. Because what is in the standard is our daily food. Or course you have to be aware that you can't only live on the new; you will starve. That is why I said you have to begin with the fact that every one of us has grown into his own world. That is our history, and that history is in part an individual, in part a social one, in part a cultural one, and in part it is of course part and parcel of the whole development of mankind. And what we have is the given, the given order. My whole point was that the only difference by which you can distinguish a work of art from the other things that are in the order is the fact that a true and great work of art is, as I put it, an epiphany of pure order in a way that you do not encounter when you go into the examples.

We have gone through a period where teaching has meant getting the historical precedents first. When I came to this country, forty and more years ago, I had never thought that historicism can go that far. When I began to teach in this country, I didn't know that things have numbers. You know: Math 243. I asked: what is it? Nobody would tell me. They would say, well, it used to be 343 but then they reduced it. They reduced it for this or that reason, and it is different from something else. They told me the whole history, who instituted it. But I could never find out what the thing was. They believe that when you have the whole history of something you have explained it, that when you know how things came to be, then you know what they are.

I think that when you deal with the work of art you are dealing with novelty, and here I am certainly not alone. There is a very fine study of novelty by Carl Hausman at Penn State on that very subject, from the philosophical point of view. The novelty of the work of art is not the novelty of what God has created out of nothing. It is the old thing in a new form. And so we do have to ask the question: what is new, why does it strike us as new, and what does the new do to us? That is not a rejection of the historical viewpoint but an anchoring of the historical viewpoint in the life of the individual, of the society, and of the work of art itself. And I need not tell you of course—because you know that better than I do—that you can write a history of Goethe interpretations, of Schiller interpretations, which is the history of something that has not changed in the cold print and yet has never been the same over any period of two or three decades.

Question by Professor Robert Scranton: I'm still not sure what you mean by creation and creativity. In art or philosophy or science or mathematics, do you mean by creativity, by creation, the process of inventing something that did not exist before, devising something that did not exist before or discovering something that people were not aware of? In other words, would you say that Euclid created geometry or invented it or discovered it?

No but I do say that the Greeks invented it. I don't think Euclid did. He didn't invent it any more than Aristotle invented philosophy. If you look at the *Poetics* of Aristotle . . . if we knew all that Aristotle had before him, we almost wouldn't need Aristotle any more. But before the Greeks you don't have that sort of thing. You have only one example, if you think about geometry and mathematics, of something like that coming into being, but in a very different form, and that is in India. You have the two great volumes of the Russian, Stcherbatsky, on Indian logic and mathematics. There you have something in an entirely different culture which resembles it. And when you think that the school of the grammarian Panini, at least 300 BC, put down the Sanskrit alphabet in the chronological order which the West discovered and used only at the end of the nineteenth century, you find that there are differences. Certain cultures do not develop certain things and others do. So it was not Euclid but it *was* the Greeks.

Follow-up question: But take the Pythagorean theorem. Didn't its truth, didn't the reality of that, precede Pythagoras?

Well, I talked about that in one lecture, and I don't mind repeating it. The Egyptians did that stuff by taking three rods of three- four- and five-unit lengths. Put them together and you've got a right angle. And they never discovered the reason why. They never went from there to the general statement of the relationship that exists between a, b and c. That is the difference.

Another follow-up: So it was the discovery of that truth that was the creation?

Well, you can say "the discovery," but it wasn't like discovering something that had always been sitting there. A mathematical theorem is not something that's out there. It's up here. It's the creation of a form that makes it possible even to ask the question. And the Greeks were great inventors of these forms.

You see, we had had myth for a long time, ages, but it was the Greeks who found a form for that myth that gave a completely new meaning to the myth itself, and that was Greek tragedy. Now, we don't have that sort of thing anywhere else. The Indians of course had plays, but they were not Greek tragedies. There is a wonderful story of Jorge Luis Borges,[21] which I used in a paper on Greek tragedy.[22] The Arab philosopher Averroës is translating Aristotle and he comes to the term "tragedy". He doesn't know how to translate it because he doesn't know what it is. He looks it up and he can't find anything. In the evening he is invited by a friend who has another guest, a traveler who has just come back from far away, from God knows where. He tells about his travels and about a strange experience somewhere in India or Egypt or China. He says it was very peculiar. There was a house and it was a peculiar house, with people sitting all around. It had a lot of doors but it had no rooms and no back side. And people would come out of the doors and they would fight each other with wooden swords and kill each other. And then the dead ones got up again and bowed and walked back. His host explained that they were acting out a story. The philosopher went home, pondering this. Suddenly he knew what tragedy was. Tragedy, he wrote is something in which many wise things are presented. The Koran is full of these wise things, so *we* don't need tragedy.

There you have a very simple contact between two cultures. And you have to say that to invent something like Greek tragedy is creative, especially in this case, because where do you get what I just called the well ordered created universe better than in Greek tragedy? Take two of them, the *Oresteia* and take *Oedipus at Colonus*. Where is Colonus? Near Athens. Oedipus is now

21. Jorge Luis Borges, "La Busca de Averroës," *Prosa Completa* (Buenos Aires: Bruguera, 1980) Vol II, 69–76. Eng. tr., "The Search of Averroës," in *Labyrinths. Selected Stories and Other Writings by Jorge Luis Borges* (New York: New Directions, augmented edition, 1964) 148–155.

22. Gregor Sebba, "Die Tragödie," *Das politische Denken der Griechen* (ed. Peter Weber-Schäfer; Munich: List, 1969) 17–47.

blind, and his death is imminent. He has been told by the gods
that where he is buried, there the blessing of the gods will be
with the people. And it is the king of Athens, Theseus, who
offers him asylum. Now comes the great scene where Oedipus,
the blind man, says: if my time has come, we will hear the
thunder of the gods. And the seeing man, the blind man, goes
down to his death as if he were led. And nobody knows where he
is buried.

And where is Colonus? It is where the *Oresteia* ends, namely,
where the Furies have driven Orestes from one place to another
and come finally to Athens. Athens gives him asylum, and now
the question is: who is right, the people, the democratic people
of Athens who gave him asylum, or the Furies whose duty it is to
punish? The goddess Athena now confronts the supreme court
of Athens with the question. The Furies make their case and
Orestes makes his case. The goddess doesn't vote (because she is
the chairman) but she proposes the democratic compromise:
Orestes will live out his life in Athens; the Furies will not per-
secute him. In return they will get something that they never had
before: a home. And where is the home? In the mountain at
Colonus. The Furies accept and say: but one of these days we will
come out of that mountain and destroy everything that is
around us.

So what do you have in these two myths by two different
poets? Aeschylus and Sophocles brought together the notion
that there are crimes so hideous that they are no longer under
human jurisdiction, but they put the criminal in the hands of the
gods. Oedipus: the two great crimes, patricide and incest, but
whoever is in the hands of the gods is sacred. The word *sacrum*
has two meanings, holy and accursed. And that is why the place
where the accursed man dies and is buried will be a sacred place:
because he is one who is in the hands of the gods. But the gods
are not only the ones who give; they are also the gods who take
away, the Erinyes. And so he is buried right where the Furies are
who are going to destroy the very things that the gods are now
giving to the city of Athens.

If you want a greater composite myth about good and bad,
right and wrong, and about things rising and falling, about
cultures, about democracy, about rights . . . no civilization that I
know has produced that, except the Greeks. But in order to do
that they had to create, out of what we now believe were ritual

dances, first, the story that is told by one actor, then the tragedy of Aeschylus, where there are two, and, with Sophocles, three, and eventually that tragedy. And that is a creation. Is that OK? No, I see Bob doesn't like it.

Dr. Scranton: At least I see what you mean.

Another question: May I put one more question? I was reminded of two categories of Aristotle. The category of nature has its laws, its structure, and its cosmos, but art is perfect, is more perfect than the natural cosmos. I have the impression that there is a quite similar idea behind your proposals: that in the art work one has to see a basic natural cosmos which perhaps may shift, like a *gestaltschnitt* shifts, into a new structure which is more perfect than the older was.

I would totally accept that, and I want to say that nothing I have said is really new. You can't say anything new any more— God be thanked. However, you can say it in a form that is renewing something old. When you speak of this perfection of the order, then I have to bring out something I mentioned, but I don't think I have made it very clear, namely, that the work of art is an epiphany of pure order, not because of what it offers but because of what it can afford not even to mention. We would all be gods if we could just be gods with a little bit of something. But when it comes to the bigger job—you know, to make something that is beyond the work of art even—then the creator too runs into these laws of nature. That is why Goethe said there are the great creators like Alexander the Great, like Julius Caesar, and like Napoleon, and they have a job to do that's given to them by nature of by the gods or by God, and when that job is done, they have to go because they have become useless. That means they have done something in reality; they have handled reality; they have produced something in reality, and it is now here, with all the imperfections that reality always has. So you can achieve perfection only by renunciation, and that is the reason why renunciation plays a tremendous part in all creative acts.